COMMON CORE
SENSE

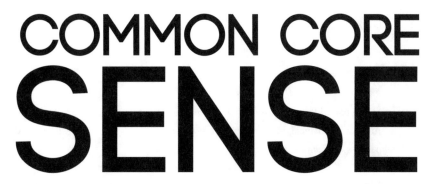

COMMON CORE SENSE

Tapping the Power of the Mathematical Practices

Christine Moynihan

Stenhouse PUBLISHERS

Portland, Maine

Stenhouse Publishers
www.stenhouse.com

Library of Congress Cataloging-in-Publication Data
Moynihan, Christine, 1951-
  Common core sense : tapping the power of the mathematical practices / Christine Moynihan.
    pages cm
  Includes bibliographical references and index.
  ISBN 978-1-62531-004-0 (pbk. : alk. paper) -- ISBN 978-1-62531-052-1 (ebook) 1. Mathematics--Study and teaching--Standards. I. Title.
  QA11.2.M686 2015
  510.71'2073--dc23
                                                        2014041910

Cover design, interior design, and typesetting by Alessandra S. Turati

Manufactured in the United States of America

PRINTED ON 30% PCW
   RECYCLED PAPER

21 20 19 18 17 16 15   9 8 7 6 5 4 3 2

To teachers everywhere who use their incredible power to bring the beauty and elegance of mathematics to those children lucky enough to be within their spheres of influence

CONTENTS

ACKNOWLEDGMENTS

I may be identified as the author of this book, but in fact, there are many who were involved in its writing. My experiences, my thoughts, my words have been shaped by the many teachers, administrators, and, most important of all, by the children who have touched me and made imprints on my life in immeasurable ways.

Special thanks go to the students, teachers, and administrators of an amazing school: the Abby Kelley Foster Charter Public School in Worcester, Massachusetts. This K–12 school of more than 1,400 students is a place where all decisions revolve around what is best for the children it serves. That message is sent clearly by Executive Director Kathleen Greenwood and is echoed by all who are part of this extraordinary place. In addition to Kathleen, my thanks go to Elementary Principal Amy Emma, who allowed me into her classrooms and supported my work in every way. I was privileged to work specifically with six teachers: Kristen Lanier (kindergarten), Brenda Stoddard (grade 1), Nancy Freud (grade 2), Kelly Connors (grade 3), Brooke Hanson (grade 4), and Shannon Murphy (grade 5). I cannot thank them enough for graciously welcoming me into their classrooms countless times, for letting me watch them in action, for granting me access to their students, and for permitting me to pick their brains while giving invaluable feedback as this book unfolded. None of this would have been possible, however, if not for the efforts of Curriculum Coordinator (K–5) Emily Jermine. She is masterful at her job and went far beyond its parameters to help me, and I simply have no words to thank her enough.

It would also be hard to give adequate thanks to Debra Shein-Gerson. Not only is Debbie an incredibly talented mathematics curriculum specialist (and a dear friend), but she is also the best sounding board I could have—always ready and willing to respond and react to my thoughts and ideas, and then talk me through the process. Additionally, I am fortunate to have others in my circle of friends whose support is unwavering and greatly appreciated—many thanks to Mimi, Blake, and Laurie.

Let it be known that I have the best editor in the world! Not only is Toby Gordon the consummate professional, but she also imbues her work with compassion and understanding in such a way that all who are guided by her are brought to a better place. I am, indeed, quite lucky. Toby is also responsible for giving me a remarkable reviewer, Kassia Omohundro Wedekind, who gives such incredible feedback that I am in her debt as well.

At the end of the day, it's all about family. My eight siblings and I grew up with unconditional love that allowed us to take risks and grow and led us to the lives we live today, still and forever connected. It almost goes without saying, but still must be said, that I could not and would not be able to do the work I do if I did not have the love of my husband and two children—Kevin, Brian, and Caitlin are the center of my world.

WHY THIS BOOK

Since the arrival of the Common Core State Standards (2010), states that have adopted the CCSS are working hard to "unpack" them. In much of my recent consulting, I have been called by many districts to "do" that, with the underlying assumption that this unpacking can be "done" in a one- or perhaps two-day professional development training session. Even with this support, however, teachers report that at times they feel overwhelmed and uncertain. Although teachers want to understand and implement the standards, making sense of them requires time and sustained support.

The purpose of this book is to make the eight Standards for Mathematical Practice more accessible to elementary teachers. My hope is for teachers to make sense of the Mathematical Practices and tap into their inherent power. Although most teachers are finding that the very structure of the Standards for Mathematical Content is detailed, focused, and specific enough to make them relatively easy to understand, greater effort needs to be placed on understanding the Standards for Mathematical Practice. To set the stage for this exploration into the Mathematical Practices, I want to highlight why they are important and how they might lead you to make some shifts in your practice, thereby activating their potential.

Before I do, however, stop for a minute and stand up right where you are. Cross your arms over the front of your body. Now reverse the way in which you have crossed your arms. It's better if you can do this with someone else present, so that that person can check to ensure that you have, indeed, done it in the opposite way. If no one else is around, stand in front of a mirror. When you are sure that you have reversed the way in which you've crossed your arms, take note of what it took to do it and how it feels. When I do this with groups of teachers, I hear that it is "hard," that they have to stop, think, and analyze how they do it at first and then list the steps in their minds, that it feels "awkward," "uncomfortable," and "challenging," and that "it takes time and planning" to accomplish the task. You probably know where I am heading with this: whenever we are asked to change something that we have done one way for a long time, it *is* hard and challenging and it *does* take time and planning and it *will* feel awkward at first. It is also critical to remember that change does *not* take place just because we say it will; it takes time, support, redirection, recommitment, and perseverance. I have used this quote for years, and although no one seems to be sure of its origin, I love it and share it with you as a way to guide your commitment to incorporating the operating principles of the Standards for Mathematical Practice into your daily teaching:

Change is a process, not an event.

So cut yourself some slack and realize that deep changes to your practice will evolve over time, accept that the road will not always be easy, and believe that your push for change will be worth the effort in the long run.

The more I work to understand the Mathematical Practices, the more I see that they transcend the teaching and learning of mathematics. Although they are housed in the CCSS for Mathematics, the Mathematical Practices apply to all content areas. They embody all that is connected to thinking—deep and substantive thinking. They foster the kind of thinking that is reflected in the work of Benjamin Bloom (1956) and his associates Lorin Anderson and David Krathwohl (Anderson et al. 2001) and ask us to immerse our students in higher-order thinking skills that involve explaining one's thinking, applying new learning, analyzing, evaluating, and creating. Further, the Mathematical Practices answer the seven "world of work survival skills" that Tony Wagner (2008) identified after speaking with more than 600 business leaders and asking them what they needed in their workers now and in the future. So although the Mathematical Practices are named "mathematical," they really are much more than that. If our students can solve problems; think both quantitatively and abstractly; build arguments that make sense; develop the capacity to listen to and learn from others' thinking; represent, model, and solve real-world problems;

and know when, why, and how to access tools and resources; if our students are efficient and accurate, and can communicate their thinking well enough so that others can follow; if they can identify and use patterns, regularities, and structures to find solutions to problems and then generalize their findings, and remain open to ideas and persevere while maintaining wonder and curiosity, then we have done our job and done it well by answering our major educational mandate: to prepare students for life beyond the school building, for life in the twenty-first century as productive and responsible workers, consumers, citizens, and caretakers of the future.

Mathematical Practices Overview

Mathematical Practice 1: Make sense of problems and persevere in solving them.

Mathematical Practice 2: Reason abstractly and quantitatively.

Mathematical Practice 3: Construct viable arguments and critique the reasoning of others.

Mathematical Practice 4: Model with mathematics.

Mathematical Practice 5: Use appropriate tools strategically.

Mathematical Practice 6: Attend to precision.

Mathematical Practice 7: Look for and make use of structure.

Mathematical Practice 8: Look for and express regularity in repeated reasoning.

Although most teachers have seen the list of Mathematical Practices, many report that they have not had much of an opportunity to explore them deeply. I think the following framework can help teachers gain a stronger foothold in their knowledge and understanding of the MPs and will provide a glimpse of how they may look in a classroom.

THE G-O-L-D FRAMEWORK

Right from the start, I have called the Mathematical Practices "gold"—something valuable and precious and absolutely critical to the development of proficient mathematical thinkers. I see each of the MPs as made up of many "nuggets" that coalesce into something bigger, with far-reaching ramifications. The further I got into my professional development work with the MPs, the more I began searching for a way to make them more comprehensible and available to teachers in the everyday moments of the classroom. I came up with a framework—something that could be used as an outline at first—and then filled it with the "stuffing," the "nuggets," that give it shape and substance.

I began to think about the acronym *GOLD* in relation to the MPs. I believe that if teachers can break apart each of the MPs in the following way, it may help them analyze each one as a separate entity, think about what this may look and sound like in classrooms, and then decide what needs to be done to support the incorporation and implementation of the MPs into daily practice. With the support of this book, it is my hope that teachers will be able to make more sense of the MPs and find the "gold" within, thereby getting to the source of the power of mathematical proficiency.

The Framework

Go for the goals: What are the major purposes of the practice?

Open your eyes and observe: What should you see students doing as they use the practice? What should you see yourself doing as a teacher?

Listen: What should you hear students saying as they use the practice? What should you hear yourself saying?

Decide what you need to do as a teacher: What actions must you put into place in order to mine the gold of the practice?

In the chapters that follow, each practice is broken into the nuggets of the framework, and we examine how each practice should look in the classroom, how it should sound, and what steps can be taken to mine its gold. We'll explore the "what" as well as the "why" of each practice and their importance. Additionally, student work samples, classroom vignettes, and thoughts from teachers throughout give a fuller view of the MPs. Chapter 9 provides some starting places to guide your steps as you continue to work to implement the Mathematical Practices more fully, with greater consistency, and deeper effect.

Teachers often find that the lines between and among the Mathematical Practices are blurred. The truth is that overlaps exist. As you read the book, you may sometimes think that what I am assigning to one MP sounds as if it can, should, and does belong to another MP. That will and should happen, as the MPs are discrete entities but do not exist in isolation. Further, as you read a classroom vignette, you may think that the scenario is giving evidence of a Mathematical Practice in addition to the one being discussed. Again, that will and should happen; just keep in mind that although a particular classroom lesson will have examples of multiple MPs, it will focus on the MP being highlighted as a dominant one in that particular vignette. Additionally, know that I have limited the number of "nuggets" within each part of the framework. There are more goals for each of the MPs than listed, but in an effort to make this as manageable as possible, I have attempted to name the most important ones, thus allowing for greater focus.

As we head into the first chapter, let me share a thought from someone who cares deeply about education in today's society. Robert John Meehan has been an educator for more than forty years and has made it his mission to share some of what happens in classrooms. This quote encapsulates what I believe is at the core of all teachers who face every day knowing that the responsibility they have is, indeed, an awesome one in every sense of the word and that their potential effect on children is limitless:

> *If your actions in the classroom inspire children to achieve more, question more, and dream more, you are indeed worthy of the title "Teacher."*

Meehan says it both succinctly and beautifully, and every committed teacher, whether aware of the quote or not, lives this every day. They are the teachers who know that every move they make should be purposeful, because each move carries power—the power to shape the learning of each and every child, the power to inspire every child to want to learn, the power to help each and every student create and fulfill dreams. It's not easy work, and there is often muddy water to go through, but if we move into the mud of the river, scoop up the nuggets, wipe away the outer muck, examine them closely, and polish each one, we can find the gold—the power—within the Mathematical Practices and move along in helping students actualize their potential.

CHAPTER 1

MATHEMATICAL PRACTICE 1:
MAKE SENSE OF PROBLEMS AND PERSEVERE IN SOLVING THEM

*By developing problem solving skills, we learn not only how to
tackle math problems, but also how to logically work our way
through any problems we may face. The memorizer can only solve
problems he has encountered already, but the problem solver can
solve problems she's never seen before. The problem solver is
flexible; she can diversify. Above all, she can create.*

—*RICHARD RUSCZYK, FOUNDER, ART OF PROBLEM SOLVING COMPANY*

OVERVIEW

What a wide-ranging view Richard Rusczyk has of problem solving!
Although many people are uncomfortable when faced with "word
problems"—problems that require more than straight computation and
are without an immediately visible solution path—some see them in the larger
context of problem solving. Among those are the authors of the Common Core,
as well as most mathematics teachers and leaders. They push forth the idea that
problem solving is at the very center of being a proficient mathematical thinker.
Being a problem solver means that one is able to analyze problems, reason
about them, build arguments that support solutions, connect them to everyday
life, use the right tools at the right moment to solve them, and be precise in
communicating how they can be solved while at the same time looking for and
using patterns and structures that are regular and repeat.

Notice anything? Of course! Being able to *make sense of problems and
persevere in solving them* is played out in each of the eight Mathematical
Practices. This first MP is the glue that holds the other MPs together and creates
an interweaving of thinking skills of the highest order. Note the word *thinking*
here, rather than *memorizing*. We are well served by committing many things
to memory, but being a good memorizer does not necessarily make one a good
problem solver. More important, however, being a good problem solver in
mathematics carries over to all areas of the curriculum, and indeed, to life in
general. When you can attack a problem with the kinds of thinking and actions

suggested in the MPs and do so without giving up, you are far more likely to succeed.

GOALS

The three major goals of this Mathematical Practice focus on students being able to

1. make meaning of the problem, understand what is being asked, and chart a general course of action;

2. develop strategies for solving problems for which little or no direction is given, possibly drawing from similar problems; and

3. demonstrate flexibility and perseverance when solving problems.

▶ Goal 1

To make meaning of the problem, understand what is being asked, and chart a general course of action (Figure 1.1)

▶ Importance of This Goal

Understanding a problem, and making good enough sense of it to know what you are being asked to find so that you can begin to solve it, seems like an obvious first step in problem solving. Even though it may be obvious, however, it is not always easy. As a young man in Budapest, George Polya found that although he was not a good memorizer, he was good at solving problems. He eventually emigrated from Budapest to the United States, where he taught at Brown and Stanford and shared with thousands of teachers through the years a simple four-step plan for solving problems (Polya 1945). He found, as many of you most likely do, that the first step, Understand the Problem, was and is a problem in and of itself. Many of us watch in frustration when a student reads a problem (quickly), pauses for perhaps three seconds, and then says one or more of the following: "I don't get it!" "This is way too hard." "I think it's impossible." "Is this addition or subtraction?"

FIGURE 1.1
Goal 1

MATHEMATICAL PRACTICE 1:
MAKE SENSE OF PROBLEMS AND PERSEVERE IN SOLVING THEM

Goal 1: Make meaning of the problem, understand what is being asked,
and chart a general course of action

G—Goal	O—Observe	L—Listen	D—Do
GOAL: *I CAN* STATEMENTS	OBSERVE STUDENTS DOING:	LISTEN FOR STUDENTS SAYING:	DECIDE WHAT TO DO
• I can explain what the problem is asking me to find. • I can retell the problem in my own words and can find which information is important to know.	• Listening to a problem and then saying it in their own words • Reading and rereading problems, determining and identifying what needs to be considered, what does not need to be considered, what needs to be found	• This problem is about how many kids are here in class today, so it can't be more than 22. • The names of the people in the family don't matter, so let's ignore that and concentrate on their heights. • Oh! This is a multistep problem, but it is more than just two steps. It will take three steps and two different operations to get the final answer. • All that matters is the number of kids who need to get on a bus and how many each bus can hold, but we have to remember that a remainder means another bus is needed, since there is no such thing as part of a person or part of a bus.	• Ask *What are you being asked to find in this problem?* *Is all the information given in the problem needed?* *What do you need to include or exclude?* *Will this problem take more than one step to solve?* *What would be a "ballpark" answer for the problem?* • Model how to think through a problem and how to read (and reread) it to find its purpose. • Define, discuss, compare, and contrast relevant versus irrelevant information. • Provide problems that are interesting, engaging, and accessible to all students and able to be differentiated easily. • Ensure there are opportunities for students to work with multistep problems that also have multiple entry points. • Stress that being a successful problem solver starts with understanding the problem completely and then being able to restate it in a way that makes sense.

This is where MP1 is critically important. When students stick with a problem longer than the initial three seconds, dive back in, determine which information is relevant, discard what is extraneous, restate the problem in their own words, frame the question within so that it makes sense to them, and then make some first attempts at deciding what course of action they might follow to find the answer to the question they have identified, they are on their way to being good problem solvers.

▶ Goal 2

To develop strategies for solving problems for which little or no direction is given, possibly drawing from similar problems (Figure 1.2)

▶ Importance of This Goal

After students have determined what they need to find to solve the problem, the issue becomes how to go about doing that. Does this sound familiar to you? As a student, you had to solve some "word problems" found on the last few pages of the chapter of your math book. If the chapter had you working on multiplying two two-digit numbers, you felt fairly confident that all you had to do when you read the problem was find two two-digit numbers and then multiply them. Although it may not be quite as obvious now, students are still often presented with problems that are somewhat routine and formulaic. (John went to the store and bought a shirt for $12.99 and a pair of socks for $4.99. How much change does he get if he pays with a twenty-dollar bill?) Not too much effort is really required to solve this. When students are presented with a problem that is not "cookie cutter" and does not have an easily discernible solution path (John goes into the store with $20.00. How many different ways can he spend it?), they often get stopped in their tracks. This is when you are most likely to hear, "I don't know what to do or where to start."

Instead, here is where you want students to believe in their own power to solve the problem if they can just get in there and muck around with it a bit. You want them to suggest the use of a strategy, put it into play, and determine if this is going to get them where they need to be. If not, then you want them to be able to decide that and then pull from their repertoire of strategies, make another plan, and follow that to see if they arrive at the solution. I believe that specific problem-solving strategies need to be taught explicitly, which

FIGURE 1.2
Goal 2

MATHEMATICAL PRACTICE 1:
MAKE SENSE OF PROBLEMS AND PERSEVERE IN SOLVING THEM

Goal 2: Develop strategies for solving problems for which little or no direction is given, possibly drawing from similar problems

G—Goal	O—Observe	L—Listen	D—Do
GOAL: *I CAN* STATEMENTS	OBSERVE STUDENTS DOING:	LISTEN FOR STUDENTS SAYING:	DECIDE WHAT TO DO
• I can make a plan. • I can plan a strategy to solve the problem.	• Using manipulatives to represent the problem situation • Considering which strategies might fit a particular problem from among a repertoire of problem-solving strategies, including mental math used to find "ballpark" (estimated) answers	• Let's draw 12 lines to show how many pencils he started with and then cross out 5 for the ones he gave away and count to see how many are left. • This is like the problem we solved last week when we made a table, except this has more parts to it. • Guess and check would take too long, so let's draw a picture first. • Let's make a quick estimate of the length of each in inches first, using what we know about the height of most doorways, then measure exactly in inches, and then centimeters, and then organize the data and compare it.	• Ask *What is your first thought about how to solve this?* *What can you tell me about the problem?* *What strategies have you used in the past that have been successful?* *How can you use what you did with [a specific previous problem] to help you with this one?* *Which strategy or strategies do you think are not good ones for this problem? Why?* • Explicitly model and teach multiple problem-solving strategies. • Provide scaffolded support rather than telling students which manipulatives to use, which strategy to use, etc. • Provide problems that could be solved in multiple ways. • Confirm that although there is usually no one best way to solve a problem, some strategies are more efficient than others within the context of specific problem situations. • Highlight the importance of dipping back into previously solved problems and adapting strategies to fit new problems.

can include drawing a picture, making a list, using a table, using objects, and making the problem simpler. The Problem Solver II series offers ten strategies that can add to the collection students are building (Hoogeboom and Goodnow 2004). Having said that, however, I make a cautionary note that the learning of specific strategies should be seen as a means to an end, not the goal itself, thus supporting the idea that strategies should be viewed as "powerful tools for mathematical thinking" (Chapin, O'Connor, and Anderson 2009, 91).

▶ Goal 3

To demonstrate flexibility and perseverance when solving problems (Figure 1.3)

▶ Importance of This Goal

Is there a teacher out there who isn't thrilled when she sees a student stick with a problem that is challenging, one that the student does not "get" right away, one that requires the student to be flexible and resilient enough to try more than one strategy? This is the student who believes, among other things, that the problem can be solved and that she is capable of solving it. Part of our work as teachers is to imbue that level of self-efficacy, a belief in one's capabilities, in all of our students. When students believe that they are up to a task, they are more likely to engage in it and stay engaged in trying to complete it, rather than pushing back from the table, both literally and figuratively, giving up on the task, and giving in to the idea that they are less than competent problem solvers. Supporting the growth of self-efficacy as a component of MP1 can only lead to a positive effect on students' development. Self-efficacy makes a difference, as "self-efficacious students show greater perseverance during adversity, are more optimistic, have less anxiety, and achieve more than do students who lack self-efficacy" (Rollins 2014, 121). Building this belief within students is absolutely critical to their success. Helping students see and believe that a little perseverance in solving math problems can and does go a long way is a win-win for all.

FIGURE 1.3
Goal 3

MATHEMATICAL PRACTICE 1:
MAKE SENSE OF PROBLEMS AND PERSEVERE IN SOLVING THEM

Goal 3: Demonstrate flexibility and perseverance when solving problems

G—Goal	O—Observe	L—Listen	D—Do
GOAL: *I CAN* STATEMENTS	OBSERVE STUDENTS DOING:	LISTEN FOR STUDENTS SAYING:	DECIDE WHAT TO DO

• I can try again and not give up if I get stuck.
 	
• I can keep trying, persevere, and find another plan to solve the problem.
	• Using a different strategy when an obstacle arises
	
	• Accessing resources when solving problems (working with a partner, trying a different manipulative, etc.)
		• This is hard—I'm stuck here, so I'm going to try something else.
		
		• I know that I have to add, but I'm not sure which numbers to use. Maybe if I use a calculator and you use a hundreds chart, we can compare.
		
		• That plan didn't work—we came up with a number that just doesn't make sense. Maybe we should draw a picture of the problem and make a chart to show our steps instead of just adding and subtracting in our heads.
		
		• This can't be right, because it's greater than what we started with, and it can't be. We must have used the wrong operation. Let's make a chart and see what we did.
			• Ask
			
			  Can you say what you know for sure about the problem?
			
			  What do you think you know?
			
			  Where are you stuck?
			
			  Can you solve this in a different way?
			
			  Can you compare two strategies for solving this problem? Is one better than the other? Why?
			
			• Model how to assess when to abandon a first (but problematic) strategy and move on to another strategy.
			
			• Outlaw "I don't get it!" and have students replace it with "This is what I know; this is where I get stuck."
			
			• Acknowledge that it can be frustrating to come to a roadblock in problem solving and that there is value in sticking with it.
			
			• Model that there are multiple solution paths to most problems.
			
			• Be explicit in how mistakes can be used to find the right solution, model how, and recognize and celebrate "good" mistakes.

CLASSROOM LESSON: GET TO WORK

▶ Bicycle Business

The context of the problem is set within a poem that details a situation in which a boy bought a bicycle, sold it, bought it back, and then sold it again. The question arises about whether or not the boy made out well in the deal. Try the problem yourself and see what you think. Although this problem certainly calls for students to make sense of the problem and to push through and solve it—MP1—it also addresses multiple MPs, as most problems do. As you work the problem yourself, take some time to think about MP2: Reason Abstractly and Quantitatively, as well as MP4: Model with Mathematics to see how these practices also come into play.

Bicycle Business

A boy bought a bicycle with fun in mind;
He paid 70 dollars and considered it a find.

No sooner was it his, when a deal came his way:
A girl offered to buy it and 90 dollars would pay.

The boy quickly agreed and completed the pact:
He knew he had done well and that was a fact.

But he soon realized he was bike-less again,
So he bought the bike back but had to pay 110!

Again to his surprise, someone offered him more,
So for a price of 130, the bike was rolled out the door.

By this time the boy was now dazed and confused—
Had he come out ahead? Did he win or did he lose?

▶ Classroom Lesson Overview—Take a Look

- Grade: 3

- Focus Content Standard(s): 3.OA.8 Solve two-step [possibly more in this case] word problems.

- Student Language: Solve problems that have more than one step.

- Focus Math Practice: MP1: Make Sense of Problems and Persevere in Solving Them.

- I Can Statement: I can retell the problem in my own words and find the information that is important to know.

- Lesson Setup:

The lesson began with three different students reading aloud from the board: the Focus Content Standard (in student language), the Focus Math Practice, and the I Can Statement.

Mrs. Connors, the classroom teacher, asked what it takes to solve a problem. The students shared that the first step is to find out "what you need to do." Mrs. Connors followed up with, "How do you figure that out?" and thus began an interchange that revolved around "finding the numbers that are important and then deciding if you have to add, subtract, multiply, or divide."

The discussion continued as the teacher asked, "Are all the numbers in a problem important?" which led to students coming to the conclusion that "just because a number is in a problem doesn't mean you have to use it." Mrs. Connors brought everyone's attention back to the "I Can" statement and asked the students to give an example of when both numbers and other kinds of information are not essential to the solving of a problem.

The teacher selected a student to read aloud the problem prompt, after which she asked all of the students to turn and talk to a neighbor about the problem. After a few moments, Mrs. Connors had students share which information was important. Next, she asked for volunteers to restate the problem in their own words.

Students were subsequently placed into pairs, as determined by the teacher. Before being sent off to work, they were reminded that they could use anything they needed to solve the problem. They were also reminded that they needed to record their solutions using words, numbers, and/or pictures (at least two of the three).

▶ Classroom Lesson Observations—Look Some More

As students set off to work, some immediately went to the class math center and picked up some "money," because they knew from the outset that using it might help them solve the problem. Most of the pairs started their work by reading the problem aloud, either taking turns reading verses or reading in unison, and some had each partner read the whole poem by him- or herself.

After the initial readings, which seemed to engage the students, it was easy to see that they were considering various strategies. A few just wanted to pull out all the numbers and add them all at once. When they realized that didn't make sense, they tried again. Some added what the boy paid out (70 and 110), figuring that he spent $180, and then adjusted with the $130 he made at the end, concluding that he lost $50 (see Donny's work in Figure 1.4). When pushed by Mrs. Connors with a guiding question about how many transactions there were in all, Donny saw that he had missed one, and he was able to make the adjustment from there.

Many students had some difficulty deciding what to do after they had finished reading the problem. Some looked around to see what other pairs were doing to see if they could mirror them. Some were ready to give up, and they actually moved away from their partners. Mrs. Connors was strategic in her timing and asked a question to offer an entry point into the problem: "What is the important information in the problem?" She allowed them to think about this and respond and then followed with, "What would this situation look like if you acted it out?" That was enough for some of the students who hadn't gotten "money" earlier to get it now. Then the pairs designated one person as the boy in the poem and acted out the problem. You can see how Trinity and Abby then mapped out how they came to a solution (see Figure 1.5).

FIGURE 1.4

Donny's work on the "Bicycle Business" problem

Name: Donny _____ Date: _____

BICYCLE BUSINESS

A boy bought a bicycle with fun in mind:
He paid 70 dollars and considered it a find.

No sooner was it his, when a deal came his way –
A girl offered to buy it and 90 dollars would pay.

The boy quickly agreed and completed the pact:
He knew he had done well and that was a fact.

But he soon realized he was bike-less again,
So he bought the bike back but had to pay 110!

Again to his surprise, someone offered him more,
So for a price of 130, the bike was rolled out the door.

By this time the boy was now dazed and confused –
Had he come out ahead? Did he win or did he lose?

~ Did the boy make a profit or did he lose money in this deal? ~
Show your work and defend your thinking.

He lost 50 dollars

```
 110
+70
─────
 180 - 130 = 50 dollars
```

FIGURE 1.5

Abby and Trinity's work on the "Bicycle Business" problem

Name: Abby and Trinity   Date: _____

BICYCLE BUSINESS

A boy bought a bicycle with fun in mind;
He paid 70 dollars and considered it a find.

No sooner was it his, when a deal came his way –
A girl offered to buy it and 90 dollars would pay.

The boy quickly agreed and completed the pact:
He knew he had done well and that was a fact.

But he soon realized he was bike-less again,
So he bought the bike back but had to pay 110!

Again to his surprise, someone offered him more,
So for a price of 130, the bike was rolled out the door.

By this time the boy was now dazed and confused –
Had he come out ahead? Did he win or did he lose?

~ Did the boy make a profit or did he lose money in this deal? ~
Show your work and defend your thinking.

bought a bike for 70$

sold it for 90$

bought a new bike for 110$

traded the bike for 130$

−70
−110

+90
+130

He won because he earned more money than he spent. He spent $180 and earned $220, so he's up $40.

CLASSROOM TEACHER REFLECTIONS — KELLY CONNORS, GRADE THREE

▶ Lesson Reflection

At first the students were excited because the problem was in a poem format. After trying to solve it, however, they became confused. About half of them had given up and were starting to get off task. When I gave them an entry point, asked them to retell the problem in their own words, and then asked which information was important to use, they were able to get back into the problem. After some were encouraged to use money and act out the scenarios, they got excited again and realized it wasn't too hard if they continued to persevere. I also saw a lot of students use tables, number lines, and some of the addition and subtraction methods they had developed and used through the year.

I loved seeing them at work. By now, near the end of the year, they finally had learned that they could come at this problem in different ways. They didn't all get the right answer, and many made some silly mistakes, but they kept trying and never gave up.

▶ MP1 Reflection

Of all the MPs, I think this is the clearest, most concise, and easiest to understand. All along, I had thought that I had a good grasp of what this MP meant and had strategies to help realize it in my classroom. What I did not do but have brought to my practice as a result of it being modeled for me, however, is to use student mistakes as a learning opportunity. One of my students had volunteered to give her answer to a problem but had come across a snag in her thinking. She was frustrated and about to stop when it was modeled for me how to capitalize upon the situation by saying, "Wow! Trinity, thank you for making that mistake and bringing it to the attention of the class. We all can learn so much from this." Trinity lit up with pleasure, and I saw the power of highlighting students' mistakes. She felt positive, and so did the rest of the class. In the past I had led discussions about how mistakes were made, but I had not held them up to the light in this way. It was a great learning experience for

Trinity, her classmates, and me. My students have become proud of their "good" mistakes and are more willing than ever to dissect them and discover where and why they went wrong. A result of this has been that they are sticking to a problem much longer than they used to and are really trying to find solutions.

COMMENTS ABOUT MP1 FROM OTHER CLASSROOM TEACHERS

Kindergarten Teacher: At the beginning of this year, I saw that most of my students thought that solving problems meant giving the right answer to an addition combination. They had been taught to memorize as the major way to solve problems. I have come to realize the importance of explicitly teaching different problem-solving strategies and then providing students with various types of problems. We, as teachers, have to *model* for our students how to solve problems and how to persevere. Once students have that strong foundation, they will begin to choose the best and most efficient ways independently. Adults are not thrown into their careers and jobs without practice, and our students deserve the same. As I have begun to focus on MP1 more fully, I believe that my students are better able to think critically, use mental math strategies they had not used before, and rely less on memorization and more on understanding what a problem is asking for them to do.

Grade Two Teacher: One of the most frustrating things I see in my classroom is the race to finish "first," especially in math. As many times as I told my students that faster isn't automatically better, it seemed to go in one ear and out the other. Before using the MPs, I would meticulously review the steps involved in solving problems: look for key information, understand the question, and so on. In a whole-group lesson, students would follow the steps wonderfully. I would feel confident sending them off for independent practice, only to find them blasting through the problem with little thought behind their actions. MP1 is about slowing down this process. It has helped me put in "speed bumps" to slow down and expand students' thought processes.

COMMENTS ABOUT MP1 FROM STUDENTS

Nathaniel, Kindergarten Student: If a problem doesn't make sense, you have to find a way to make it make sense.

Glenda, Grade Three Student: [to a classmate who had just said, "I can't do this, it's too hard!"] Hey! You can't say that! You know you need to persevere!

Francesca, Grade Four Student: If you don't persevere, you won't do well in school, and you'll get stuck doing a job that you don't really want.

MATHEMATICAL PRACTICE 2:
REASON ABSTRACTLY
AND QUANTITATIVELY

One can always reason with reason.

—HENRI BERGSON, FRENCH PHILOSOPHER

OVERVIEW

It sounds so simple and logical that you can make sense of anything by applying reasoning to it. Sherlock Holmes, so famous for using both deductive and inductive reasoning to solve mysteries, embodied this idea. Although our students are not being asked to solve mysteries, they are being asked to apply logic and reasoning to gain understanding of problems that may not yet be within their grasp. The abstract thinking involved in solving word problems can be challenging for students. How can they take a situation presented in words and represent it quantitatively with numbers and symbols? Conversely, how can students take a number sentence, an equation, an expression, or a formula and move from this quantitative form to an abstract form by creating a real-life situation that would result in the need for such a quantitative representation? Neither is easy—but both are important.

I remember when I was being taught to divide with fractions and we were told, "Yours is not to reason why; just invert and multiply." I know the teacher was trying to help us by giving us a way to remember *how* to divide with fractions, but we had no idea why we were doing so. Think about that for a minute now. Do you know why this works? Can you give mathematical evidence that is backed up with logic and reasoning about how and why this leads to the right answer when you divide two-thirds by three-fourths? Can you set ⅔ ÷ ¾ into a real-life context? Many of us were robbed of the chance to learn at an early age how to reason both abstractly and quantitatively. MP2 is asking us not to allow that to happen to this generation of students.

GOALS

The three major goals of this Mathematical Practice focus on students being able to

1. understand that situations expressed in word problems (abstract) can be represented with numbers (quantitative) and vice versa;

2. develop a strong number sense as well as gain a sense of the quantities embedded within problem contexts, the relationships between them, and how they affect the problem situation; and

3. engage in the "contexts": decontextualize (translate from words to numbers), contextualize (probe for sense-making as work progresses), and recontextualize (ensure that final answer fits into original problem and makes sense).

▶ Goal 1

To understand that situations expressed in word problems (abstract) can be represented with numbers (quantitative) and vice versa (Figure 2.1)

▶ Importance of This Goal

Many students have had the experience of feeling overwhelmed by even a few sentences that describe a problem and giving up before they even try, convinced that the problem is "too confusing." This is when they just want to be told what to do and then happily go about doing the work—usually the computation needed to get the answer. I am reminded of the old proverb, coined by Anne Isabella Thackeray Ritchie in her novel *Mrs. Dymond* (1885), "If you give a man a fish, you feed him for a day; if you teach a man to fish, you feed him for a lifetime." It is certainly more expeditious in the moment to tell students what they need to do. Who among us isn't tempted to do that sometimes? We are seemingly always running against the clock. There are also times when we want to do so because our innate need to nurture takes over and we don't want our students to feel less than adequate. In the long run, however, we all recognize that once students accept that somewhere in the jumble of the words in a problem there lies a way to make sense of the problem and build a model of it,

FIGURE 2.1
Goal 1

MATHEMATICAL PRACTICE 2:
REASON ABSTRACTLY AND QUANTITATIVELY

Goal 1: Understand that situations expressed in word problems (abstract)
can often be represented with numbers (quantitative) and vice versa

G—Goal	O—Observe	L—Listen	D—Do
GOAL: *I CAN* STATEMENTS	OBSERVE STUDENTS DOING:	LISTEN FOR STUDENTS SAYING:	DECIDE WHAT TO DO
• I can connect numbers with words and words with numbers. • I can use both numbers and words to show problem situations.	• Reasoning about numbers and their relationships • Applying understanding of the relative magnitude of numbers, depending on the context • Using objects, whiteboards, paper and pencil, etc., to write a number expression and/or sentence that matches a problem situation • Using objects, whiteboards, paper and pencil, etc., to represent a context for a given number expression and/or sentence	• Double 2 is 4 and double 4 is 8, so double 5 is the same as 5 + 5, and that's 10. • One hundred can be big and 100 can be small. A hundred pieces of candy is a lot of candy for one person, but it is a small amount if you have 200 people. • For 9 − 7 = 2, I made 9 birds and then crossed off 7 for the ones that flew away. That leaves 2 without crosses, and that's the answer. • A situation that would make me have to multiply 2 and 2¼ would be if I am making something that calls for 2¼ cups of sugar and I want to double the recipe.	• Ask *What is the meaning of the numbers in this problem?* *Why (when) would you ever have to do this particular computation?* *Can you represent this problem in a different way?* *Where else would you see numbers like this?* *Can you describe your steps in this problem in both words and numbers?* *Can you relate this problem situation to another one that is similar?* • Plan time for student-to-teacher dialogue as students explain how the mathematics they did works (prompted by your probing questions). • Plan time for student-to-student dialogue as they share and justify their thinking. • Model how you interpret a problem and how you move from the abstract (words) to the quantitative (numbers/symbols). • Give ample and consistent opportunities for students to engage in solving problems and then sharing how they moved to and from the abstract to the quantitative and vice versa. • Model how you can construct a context (abstract) for a mathematical representation (numbers/symbols).

and that they are capable of finding it with some scaffolding and practice, they are better served both in the moment and in the future.

Students take a major step forward in being able to reason both abstractly and quantitatively when they understand what they are being asked to find, say it in their own words, and then translate those words into numbers and symbols. I underscore the "translate" part with students because this suggests a connecting of words to numbers and symbols, as well as connecting actions within the problem to numbers and symbols in a methodical manner, doing so in "chunks," so to speak. Of course it takes root with students as they see it modeled by you as well as by their peers. It also helps when students engage in dialogue as they share what they are thinking and justify what they have done.

▶ Goal 2

To develop a strong number sense as well as gain a sense of the quantities embedded within problem contexts, the relationships between them, and how they affect the problem situation (Figure 2.2)

▶ Importance of This Goal

Who doesn't agree with the idea that all students must develop a strong sense of number? Of course, we all agree, but what may differ is our understanding of what number sense is, of what having a sense of number means. Although there are many definitions out there, one that has been around for a while and continues to be used comes from Francis "Skip" Fennell and Theodore Landis, who, in a chapter in *Windows of Opportunity: Mathematics for Students with Special Needs*, say succinctly that number sense is "an awareness and understanding about what numbers are, their relationships, their magnitude, the relative effect of operating on numbers, including the use of mental mathematics and estimation" (1994, 187). They, like many others, urge elementary teachers especially to understand that a strong number sense equals a strong foundation for reasoning and that this is a component essential to mathematical proficiency through middle school, high school, and beyond. This is supported in the series of books edited by Timothy Kanold about using professional learning communities as a way to bring the Common Core to life. The series' authors maintain that number sense can empower students in a minimum of six ways with the ability to express interpretations about numbers, apply relationships

FIGURE 2.2
Goal 2

MATHEMATICAL PRACTICE 2:
REASON ABSTRACTLY AND QUANTITATIVELY

Goal 2: Develop a stronger number sense as well as gain a sense of the quantities embedded within problem contexts, the relationships between them, and how they affect the problem situation

G—Goal	**O—Observe**	**L—Listen**	**D—Do**
GOAL: *I CAN* STATEMENTS	OBSERVE STUDENTS DOING:	LISTEN FOR STUDENTS SAYING:	DECIDE WHAT TO DO
• I can use what I know about numbers to solve problems. • I can represent problems with equations using known numbers and variables.	• Comparing numbers and sets to show which is greater, less, or equal (with counters, ten frames, etc.) • Exploring different ways to add and subtract • Using known number relationships to solve more complex computations • Making hypotheses about the answer, given the numbers and operations involved	• When I line up the 12 red cubes against the 10 yellow cubes, it shows that 12 is greater than 10. I also know it because 12 is a full ten frame and 2 more. • I need to find the difference between 72 and 125, so my question is 72 plus what is 125? • Four times 15 is the same as 2 times 15 done twice, so $4 \times 15 = 2 \times 15 + 2 \times 15$. • We are dividing an even number by an even number, so the answer should be even, shouldn't it?	• Ask *Do these numbers make sense in this problem?* *Do you have an idea of what the answer will be?* *What is unknown?* *What would happen if we double the numbers involved in the problem? If we double just one of them?* *Are the numbers in the problem relatively large or relatively small?* • Provide time for students to "play" with numbers, decomposing and recomposing in multiple ways (for example, the number of the day, the number of days in school, or a number from current events). • Deliberately highlight the numbers we see at home and in the world at large, and discuss how we use numbers, where we see them, etc. • Explore numbers within the context of everyday classroom life. (How much time do we have left in math? Will that be enough to . . . ?). • Present multiple opportunities for students to deepen their number sense in ways that force them to interpret numbers and to make conjectures about their relative magnitude.

between numbers, recognize magnitude of numbers, compute, make decisions involving numbers, and solve problems (Kanold 2012, 33–34).

What is important to remember about this component of MP2 is that number sense *is* learnable, that it *is* within the reach of all students. The seeds can be planted from the earliest stages of development and fostered all the way through school. When students are given opportunities to play around with numbers, to compose, decompose, and recompose numbers in multiple ways, they begin to see the relationships and connections between and among numbers. Yes, 426 can be represented as 4 hundreds, 2 tens, and 6 ones, but it can also be thought of as 3 hundreds, 12 tens, and 6 ones, as well as 200 plus 200 plus 20 plus 6, and myriad other ways. Thinking about numbers in multiple ways leads to being able to compute in multiple ways—ways that make sense based on the context. When students have played with numbers enough, they develop an understanding of their relative magnitude and can reasonably assert that at times, 100 is too large a number for a problem situation, and at other times too small.

▶ Goal 3

To engage in the "contexts": decontextualize (translate from words to numbers), contextualize (probe for sense-making as work progresses), and recontextualize (ensure that the final answer fits into original problem and makes sense) (Figure 2.3)

▶ Importance of This Goal

As students get into a problem, they must begin to build a chain of reasoning that can get them to the solution. This chain of reasoning doesn't just jump out; it requires an initial structuring of steps (decontextualizing), then working toward the solution while checking progress along the way (contextualizing), followed by making sure that the solution one has found really fits back into the problem (recontextualizing). What is frustrating for many students is that sometimes it is necessary to retrace—or even rework—steps. I agree with Cathy Seeley, who finds that this component is a critical one: "One of the most interesting aspects of Standard for Mathematical Practice 2 is the emphasis on students being able to move back and forth while solving a contextual problem between a situation and the mathematical representation of the situation" (2014,

FIGURE 2.3
Goal 3

MATHEMATICAL PRACTICE 2:
REASON ABSTRACTLY AND QUANTITATIVELY

Goal 3: Engage in the "contexts": decontextualize (translate from words to numbers), contextualize (probe for sense-making as work progresses), and recontextualize (ensure that final answer fits into original problem and makes sense)

G—Goal	O—Observe	L—Listen	D—Do
GOAL: *I CAN* STATEMENTS	OBSERVE STUDENTS DOING:	LISTEN FOR STUDENTS SAYING:	DECIDE WHAT TO DO
• I can use numbers and words to find answers that make sense. • I can make a plan from a problem situation, check work along the way, and make sure the answer makes sense.	• Drawing pictures, using objects, using counting strategies, etc., to uncover the numerical meaning of a problem context • Pausing at points to go back and forth from the quantitative representation to the problem context, checking for sense • Explaining their work as they proceed through the problem • Checking to make sure the final answer makes sense and fits into the original problem situation	• I know we are adding three numbers to find all the cookies the kids have, because there are three kids. • Let's look at our picture, starting at the first leg of the race and making sure our numbers match the drawing. • We have to know how many people got part of the inheritance, so let's draw a chart and then check back to see what fraction each person got. • Two hundred thousand works, because when you double 25,000, you get 50,000, and when you double again, you get $200,000.	• Ask *Can you tell why you wrote that number sentence, equation, etc., for this problem?* *What did you find in the problem that helps you have an idea what the answer will be?* *Stop after your first step. Can you tell your partner how you know you are on the right path?* *Did you have enough think time?* *What does it mean when you say that your answer makes sense?* • Model with various types of problems how to decontextualize, contextualize, and recontextualize. • Be overt in using "wait" time, showing students the value of having time to think. • Scaffold—resist the urge to help students by telling them what they need to do. • Encourage students to do "think-alouds" as they engage in solving problems. • Ask probing questions—questions that require more than one-word answers.

273). I love that she calls this process the ability to "zoom in and zoom out" as well as move "back and forth and in and out." As always, it is beneficial for you to model how engaging in this can be done and then have students model for each other as well.

Decontextualize by

- identifying relevant information within a problem context by stripping away extraneous information;

- translating relevant information into quantitative values; and

- constructing number sentences using quantitative relationships.

Contextualize by

- monitoring work along the way to gain a sense of progress toward solution;

- probing to check that interim steps toward solution make sense and align with overall context; and

- using properties of operations flexibly toward solution.

Recontextualize by

- checking to see if the answer makes sense quantitatively;

- verifying units of measure; and

- circling back to the problem context to ensure the answer connects with the context.

CLASSROOM LESSON—GET TO WORK

▶ Heads, Shoulders, Knees, and Toes

This problem revolves around the childhood favorite song of the same name. It is a natural for a math problem, especially when set in a classroom environment. The obvious question is *How many heads, shoulders, knees, and toes are there?* A bonus is how easily this can be differentiated: *How many heads, shoulders, knees, and toe are there in the class? How many in your group? What is the difference between your group and someone else's? How many heads and toes are there?* Possibilities abound for ways to modify this problem to meet and challenge multiple levels of readiness.

▶ Classroom Lesson Overview—Take a Look

- Grade: 1

- Focus Content Standard(s): 1.OA.1 Use addition to solve word problems. 1.NBT.4 Add within 100 using concrete models or drawings or strategies . . . and relate the strategy to a written method and explain the reasoning used.

- Student Language: Use addition to solve word problems and show my reasoning in words, pictures, and/or numbers.

- Focus Math Practice: MP2: Reason Abstractly and Quantitatively

- I Can Statement: I can connect numbers with words and words with numbers.

- Lesson Setup:

The lesson began with Mrs. Stoddard, the classroom teacher, leading a discussion about the use of math in our everyday lives. Students shared several ways in which they use math both in and out of school.

Mrs. Stoddard then had the students stand in a circle and led the class in singing and acting out "Heads, Shoulders, Knees, and Toes." She followed by asking the students if they could see any math in that activity. Several responded that they could count how many heads were in the class, some said that the number of toes could be found, and so forth.

The lesson continued with three students reading aloud from the board the Focus Content Standard(s) in Student Language, the Focus Math Practice, and the I Can Statement.

Mrs. Stoddard then asked if there were any tools that might be helpful in finding the number of the situations they had suggested. Students suggested ten frames, counters, and base ten blocks, among others. Mrs. Stoddard spoke about the importance of using words, numbers, and/or pictures as ways students could share their reasoning.

Students were placed into partner groups (as determined by the teacher). They were asked to find the answers to the questions as presented on the worksheet. Differentiations were made accordingly: some students completed the task for two students per group, some for a group of three, and some for a group of four.

▶ Classroom Lesson Observations—Look Some More

Once they set off to work in their smaller groups, the students seemed excited about digging in to solve the problem. Mrs. Stoddard had set up workstations for the groups in advance and provided an array of tools for them to use. It was interesting to watch who gravitated toward counters, whiteboards for drawing, ten frames, base ten blocks, a hundreds board, and so on. It was also interesting to watch and listen as they decided as a group which tool might be the best one to use.

Some groups were very straightforward in their approach. One group of four collectively counted out four counters for their heads and kept them separate from the next collection they made for their eight shoulders. They next counted out forty counters. Each student counted out ten for his or her own toes and placed them in a group, and then they counted out the last group for their eight knees. They then proceeded to meld the groups together, adding as they merged each group. See Alby's work (Figure 2.4) as a representation of their reasoning. When Mrs. Stoddard asked them why they solved it that way, group members responded with answers such as, "We knew we could be exact this way and not make a mistake."

FIGURE 2.4
Alby's work on the "Head, Shoulders, Knees, and Toes" problem

Name: Alby _____ Date: 6/5/14 _____

Heads, Shoulders, Knees & Toes

How many heads, shoulders, knees & toes are in your group?

Show your work using numbers, words, pictures.

- My group has ___4___ people in it.

- There are __60__ heads, shoulders, knees and toes in the group.

- I can prove it by showing my thinking.

~~~~~~

$$30 + 30 = 60$$

Vivian's group had each member draw on their whiteboards either the heads, shoulders, knees, or toes. They then added heads and shoulders. ("We just knew that 4 plus 8 is 12 and then we added 8 to 12, and then 40 to 20 and got our answer."). (See Figure 2.5.) Briana's group used the ten frames. They shared with Mrs. Stoddard that they started with the toes and "filled in four complete frames first. Then we knew that the eight shoulders and eight knees together make sixteen, and that is one whole ten frame and six on another. Then there are the four heads, so if we added them in order, we got sixty in all." (See Figure 2.6.)

CLASSROOM TEACHER REFLECTIONS — BRENDA STODDARD, GRADE ONE

▶ Lesson Reflection

We had fun doing this lesson right from the start. It was easy to engage the students immediately through singing and acting out something familiar to them. We are always telling our children that math is all around them, and this was a good way to prove that. As is always my practice, I had prepared for the group work in advance in such a way that many tools would be available to them. I had also been strategic in the creation of the groups so that the students were more likely to collaborate with one another.

As I walked around and interacted with the groups, I was able to see that even though I had expected that many groups would solve the problem in the same way, that was not the case. I saw students take the time to stop and reason out the problem and keep checking back to see if their representations matched. As a result of this checking, several mistakes were found and then corrected. I particularly liked how the ways they showed both their quantitative and abstract reasoning were varied.

FIGURE 2.5

Vivian's group's work on the "Head, Shoulders, Knees, and Toes" problem

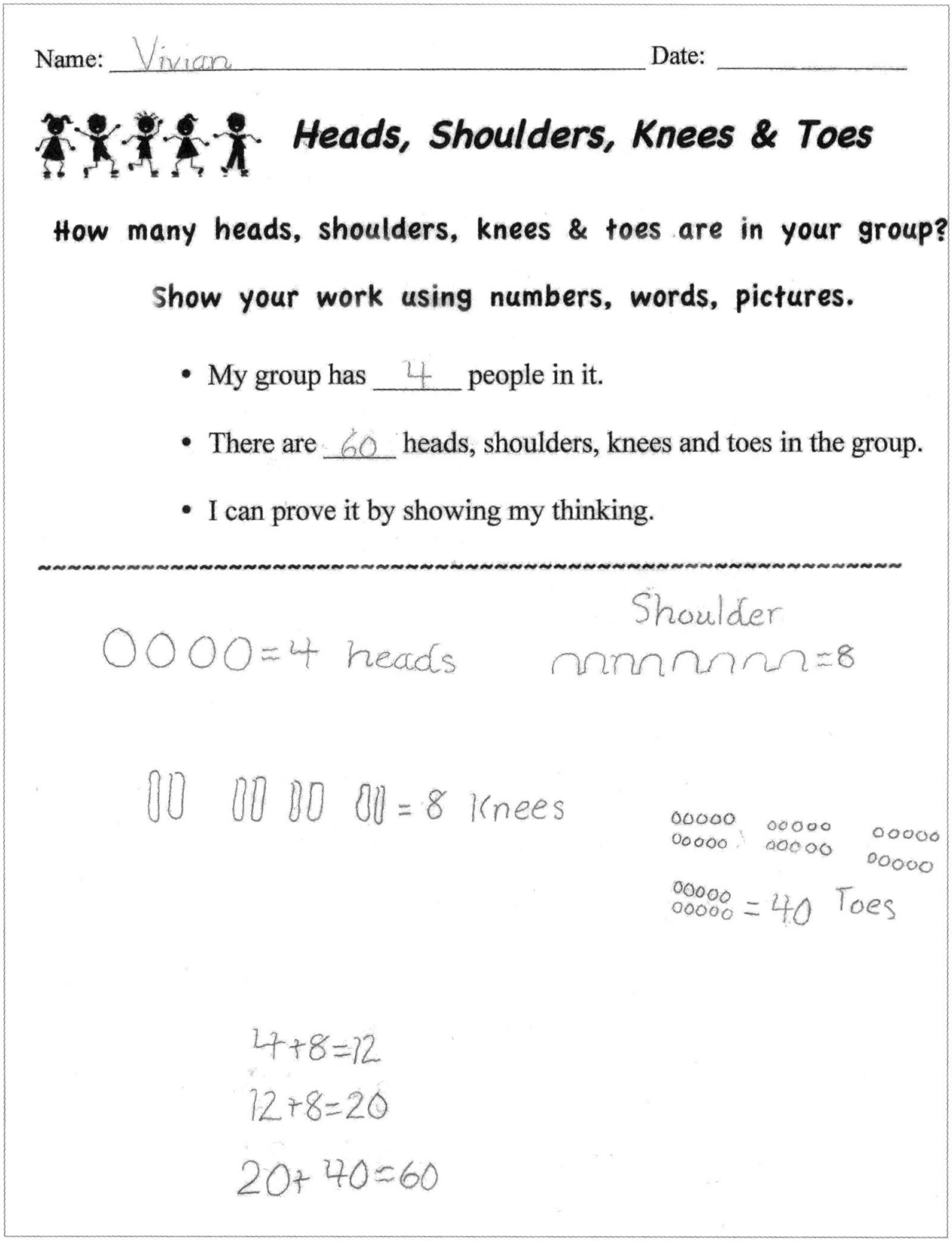

Name: Vivian _____ Date: _____

𐀀 Heads, Shoulders, Knees & Toes

How many heads, shoulders, knees & toes are in your group?

Show your work using numbers, words, pictures.

- My group has ___4___ people in it.

- There are ___60___ heads, shoulders, knees and toes in the group.

- I can prove it by showing my thinking.

~~~~~~

OOOO = 4 heads

Shoulder

ᴖᴖᴖᴖᴖᴖᴖᴖ = 8

ΙΙ ΙΙ ΙΙ ΙΙ = 8 Knees

00000 00000 00000
00000 00000 00000
00000
00000 = 40 Toes

4+8=12
12+8=20
20+40=60

FIGURE 2.6

Briana's group's work on the "Head, Shoulders, Knees, and Toes" problem

Name: _____ Briana _____ Date: _____

Heads, Shoulders, Knees & Toes

How many heads, shoulders, knees & toes are in your group?

Show your work using numbers, words, pictures.

- My group has ___4___ people in it.
- There are _60_ heads, shoulders, knees and toes in the group.
- I can prove it by showing my thinking.

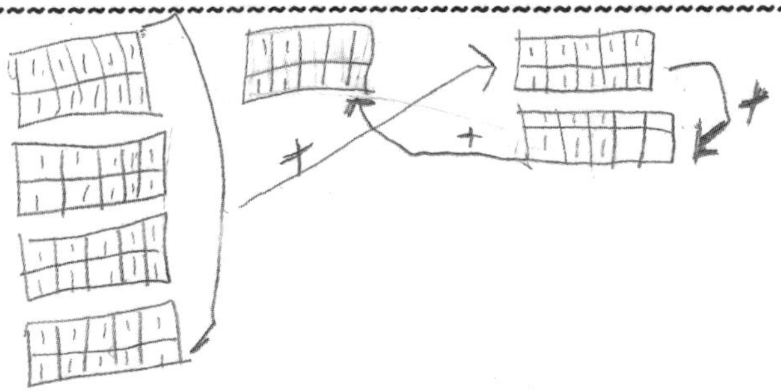

$$40 + 10 = 50$$
$$50 + 6 = 56$$
$$56 + 4 = 60$$

▶ MP2 Reflection

At the beginning of the year, I really didn't know much of anything about the Mathematical Practices. I did know that they existed and were part of the Common Core, but I was unsure of anything further than that. I have begun to have a better understanding but am still unsure of how I will ever get my head around all of this. One thing that has helped is that I can see how integrating the MPs into my practice will result in a better way of learning and thinking about math. I can now see them as a guide to helping students become better mathematicians. I see MP2 as especially useful in supporting students as they look for the practical applications of math, of how to make connections between words and numbers in problem situations, to use those relationships to make meaning. I want to continue to deepen my understanding of this particular MP, as well as all of the others, and then apply that to my daily teaching. I would like the inclusion of the MPs to be second nature to me, and I realize that this will take time and practice.

COMMENTS ABOUT MP2 FROM OTHER CLASSROOM TEACHERS

Grade Three Teacher: This Mathematical Practice is one I need to dig into more. I have an overall idea of what it is—reasoning through both an abstract lens and a quantitative one—but I definitely need to get to a deeper level of what exactly it means and how I can provide enough opportunities for my students to do it. This one is going to take some time.

Grade Five Teacher: This MP sounds relatively simple—just four words— but it's not as easy to understand as it looks. When I first read this one, I immediately thought this was something I already did, and maybe I do to some degree. I don't think, however, that I have stressed enough to my students the importance of stepping back and seeing the big picture as they are working on a problem. I pretty much had them check after they finished to see if the way they solved it and their answer made sense. I think I have to spend more time helping my kids see why they should be doing this at points throughout their work and not just at the end.

COMMENTS ABOUT MP2 FROM STUDENTS

Julio, Grade One Student: I know I need to make sure that my drawing shows how I got the answer because it shows my thinking. I sometimes put the total on the top and the parts on the bottom and make sure they go with the problem.

Ayla, Grade Four Student: This Math Practice is about going back and forth from the problem to your work and seeing if what you are doing makes sense. It isn't always easy.

Victoria, Grade Five Student: Paying attention to what the problem is saying and how I show—represent—my work and how they connect is what's important. This is challenging, and sometimes I have to make many adjustments.

MATHEMATICAL PRACTICE 3:
CONSTRUCT VIABLE
ARGUMENTS AND
CRITIQUE THE
REASONING OF OTHERS

Be able to defend your arguments in a rational way. Otherwise all you have is an opinion.

—MARILYN VOS SAVANT

OVERVIEW

The foundation of this MP lies within one of the five Process Standards set forth by the National Council of Teachers of Mathematics: communication. It is widely accepted that when you explain something to someone else, you must think about it in a deeper, more detailed way. By communicating something, even something as simple as giving someone directions to somewhere familiar to you (in the pre-GPS days), you must stop and consider your options, make a visual map for yourself first, chart out the steps, be explicit in your choice of words, consider modifications as you go along, and then review your directions to see if they are correct, cohesive, complete, and make sense to both you and the person to whom you are giving them.

NCTM maintains that communication is one of the most critical components of mathematical proficiency and views it as a key element in students grappling with and then coming to understand mathematical ideas and principles; when students communicate their thinking, "ideas become objects of reflection, refinement, discussion, and amendment" (2000, 60), serving to make them stronger. Further, NCTM maintains that when our students "are challenged to think and reason about mathematics and to communicate the results of their thinking to others orally or in writing, they learn to be clear and convincing" (2000, 60), which moves the communication from an opinion to a valid argument.

GOALS

The three major goals of this Mathematical Practice focus on students being able to

1. believe that mathematics can be explained in a logical, mathematically sound manner—that there is no "magic" in mathematics;

2. accept that *viable* explanations of mathematical thinking must be organized, reasonable, justifiable, and laden with proof; and

3. accept that receiving feedback on their mathematical arguments from both teachers and students can deepen understanding and improve thinking and that understanding the reasoning of others can do the same.

▶ Goal 1

To believe that mathematics can be explained in a logical, mathematically sound manner—that there is no "magic" in mathematics (Figure 3.1)

▶ Importance of This Goal

We have all had students who proudly proclaim, "I found a trick," or "My dad showed me a trick to do this faster." These phrases are like fingernails on a chalkboard and almost make me shudder, for simply put, there are *no* tricks in mathematics, and there is *no* magic in mathematics (other than the way it can create beauty and wonder). Try this with either students or adults:

What is 3 times 10?

What is 6 times 10?

How about 8 times 10?

The correct answers are usually given quickly and with conviction and confidence. Then ask, "How do you know?" and the response will most likely be a variation of, "The trick is that you just add a zero." First of all, it is *not* a trick. A zero is put in the ones place and the other digit shifts to the tens place for a valid reason. Second, you are not *adding* zero, for zero added to a number

FIGURE 3.1
Goal 1

MATHEMATICAL PRACTICE 3:
CONSTRUCT VIABLE ARGUMENTS AND CRITIQUE
THE REASONING OF OTHERS

Goal 1: Believe that everything in mathematics can be explained in a logical, mathematically sound manner—that there is no "magic" in mathematics

G—Goal	O—Observe	L—Listen	D—Do
GOAL: *I CAN* STATEMENTS	OBSERVE STUDENTS DOING:	LISTEN FOR STUDENTS SAYING:	DECIDE WHAT TO DO
• I can explain my thinking and why it works. • I can explain and prove how and why my thinking makes sense.	• Using concrete and pictorial tools (such as objects, drawings, etc.) as well as definitions and principles and acting on them to prove number and operational basics such as ~ the commutative property; ~ how 10 more or 10 less than a number can be found by changing the digit in the tens place; ~ how the "same change" method works for subtraction; ~ how two fractions are equivalent; and ~ why counting and adding the number of places behind the decimal points of two numbers being multiplied works in determining the number of places in the product	• When I count by tens on the hundreds chart from 25, the next is 35. The 5 ones are the same—just the tens changed—so instead of 2 tens, there are 3 tens. • Look on this number line. If I'm looking for the difference between 78 and 29, I can add 1 to 29 to move to 30, but I made the distance 1 shorter, so I have to make it 1 bigger at the 78 end, by adding 1 and moving that to 79. Now it's easy to see that 30 up to 79 is 49. • Since 6 triangles cover a hexagon, each is $\frac{1}{6}$ and 3 make $\frac{3}{6}$, which is half of a hexagon. They cover a trapezoid, so a trapezoid is also $\frac{1}{2}$. • I know that the answer to 26.2 and 4.6 will be out to the hundredths place because tenths are being multiplied by tenths and $\frac{1}{10}$ of $\frac{1}{10}$ is $\frac{1}{100}$. Let me show you with the blocks and on paper.	• Ask *Why?* *What would happen if . . . ?* *What helps you prove that your thinking is correct?* *How else could you explain your thinking?* *What math does someone need to know to understand your thinking?* • Discuss the meaning of the word *trick* as something meant to deceive, a ruse, etc. • Outlaw the word *trick* in reference to math. • Send this same message to parents (via back-to-school nights, family letters, etc.). • Constantly ask, Why did you do this? Why do you think this would work? Why did this not work? Why do you think the answer will be larger [smaller] than . . . ? • Insist on pushing past Show and Tell to TSS: Tell, Show, and Support (**Tell** what you did, **Show** how you did it, and **Support** why you did it).

results in the original number (this example, as you can see, also applies to MP6 in terms of being precise with language). An explanation such as this—just add a zero if you are multiplying by 10, two zeroes if you are multiplying by 100, and so on—robs students of the chance to see the connection between the action and multiplying by powers of 10. Noticing the pattern of the number ending in zero may be a starting point for students, but their exploration and explanation should not end here. When I hear students say, "Multiplying 3 by 10 means that there are 3 tens instead of 3 ones, and the 3 moves to the tens place; the 3 is more powerful now because it has increased by a power of 10," I can see the mathematical foundation being laid for them to take it to the next level and apply that logic to multiplying by 100 and on from there.

▶ Goal 2

To accept that *viable* explanations of mathematical thinking must be organized, reasonable, justifiable, and laden with proof (Figure 3.2)

▶ Importance of This Goal

Many times students believe that simply listing the steps they used to solve a problem is a way to explain and justify their thinking. In reality, however, telling and showing ≠ proving and justifying. Something is lost when students arrive at a correct solution, yet can tell only *what* they did to get there and not *why* they did what they did. At the heart of mathematics and all sciences is the posing of ideas and then either proving or disproving them on the basis of laws, principles, definitions, properties, theorems, and so on, so that other people can follow the chain of reasoning. The authors of the Common Core were strategic in using the adjective *viable* in the naming of this MP. From the French *vie*—life— *viable* means "capable of living." A mathematical argument is capable of living only if it is based on truths that connect and lead one to an understanding that is provable. "Much of the work of mathematicians involves arguing to prove hypotheses true or false. The kind of arguments mathematicians make consist of reasoned steps that lead logically to a conclusion in a mathematically valid way" (Seeley 2014, 280). Moving students away from a simple recitation of their steps toward providing a trail of their reasoning that creates a path others can follow is the focus of this component of MP3.

FIGURE 3.2
Goal 2

MATHEMATICAL PRACTICE 3:
CONSTRUCT VIABLE ARGUMENTS AND
CRITIQUE THE REASONING OF OTHERS

Goal 2: Accept that *viable* explanations of mathematical thinking must be organized, reasonable, justifiable, and laden with proof

G—Goal	O—Observe	L—Listen	D—Do
GOAL: *I CAN* STATEMENTS	OBSERVE STUDENTS DOING:	LISTEN FOR STUDENTS SAYING:	DECIDE WHAT TO DO
• I can explain my thinking so others can understand. • I can give an explanation that is organized, full of proof, and easy to follow.	• Checking their work (done with objects, on whiteboards, etc.) to see if it makes sense to themselves • Turning and talking—explaining their work to others • Working individually, with a partner, and/or in small groups to provide evidence based on mathematical reasoning that supports a conjecture and makes sense to others • Ensuring that they can convince themselves that their thinking is plausible, can convince someone who agrees with their conjecture, and can try to convince someone who does not agree with them	• When I said it out loud to myself, I got confused, so I have to start over. • Seventy-nine plus 12 was easy after I broke 12 into 10 and 2. I did it first on the hundreds chart and started at 79, jumped down a 10 to 89, and then counted 2 more to get 91. • We know that adding two even numbers equals an even number, two odds equal an even number, and one odd and one even equal an odd, but it will be different in multiplication because . . . Let's make a chart, fill in some numbers, find the answers, and then show how this matches our thinking. • This makes sense to me. Let me explain it to you, and then you can explain it to me and see if it still makes sense. Then . . .	• Ask *Why is it good to go through your explanation a few times?* *What is the strongest part of your mathematical thinking?* *How would you change your argument for a younger student?* *What was hard for you to explain? Why?* *What was easy for you to explain? Why?* • Model how to give an explanation that is organized, reasonable, justifiable, and laden with proof. • Highlight the terms *reasoned* and *reasonable* and promote them as benchmarks for viability. • Provide opportunities for students to critique your explanations in which there are flaws. • Provide opportunities for students to look and listen for similarities between their thinking and that of others. • Provide opportunities for students to look and listen for differences between their thinking and that of others.

▶ Goal 3

To accept that receiving feedback on their mathematical arguments from both teachers and students can deepen understanding and improve thinking and that understanding the reasoning of others can do the same (Figure 3.3)

▶ Importance of This Goal

I am sure that you have watched students as they set about solving problems that involve more than one simple step. Most read and often reread the problem, and some even read it aloud as they let the basics of the problem swirl around them. They may go and get some manipulatives and use them to act out the actions of the problem, or they may draw a picture and then get an answer that seems correct. You can surmise that many of them have constructed some sort of an internal justification along the way for what they did and why they did it. Some may even sub-vocalize their reasoning, talking aloud quietly, mostly to themselves. The ante is raised, however, when they are asked to externalize their reasoning and explain, support, and justify it to others. There are two basic levels to this externalization: presenting their thinking to a teacher and presenting it to peers. It has been my experience that students often find it easier to convince a teacher that their reasoning works, because the teacher knows the correct answer, knows many of the pathways of reasoning that can be used to get to the answer, and is adept at filling in gaps in students' explanations. It is more difficult for most students to convince peers of their reasoning.

The classroom environment and the norms with which it has been built play a significant role in the success of this component of MP3. The expectation that explanations of one's thinking are the norm and that questioning is done in a respectful way that engages all students and the teacher as well goes a long way toward achieving the kind of interactive mathematical discussions that yield positive results. When students perceive the classroom community as safe, they are more likely to share their reasoning and strategies, even if they are not completely formed. Many are accustomed to having the teacher ask, "Why did you do this?" and do not feel threatened, viewing it as an opportunity to expand and substantiate their thinking. When this extends to peers, it is more likely that the classroom will be filled with true discussions, real conversations through which students "can clarify their own thinking and learn from others" (Chapin, O'Connor, and Anderson 2009, 5).

FIGURE 3.3
Goal 3

MATHEMATICAL PRACTICE 3: CONSTRUCT VIABLE ARGUMENTS AND CRITIQUE THE REASONING OF OTHERS

Goal 3: Accept that receiving feedback on their mathematical arguments from both teachers and students can deepen understanding and improve thinking and that understanding the reasoning of others can do the same

G—Goal	O—Observe	L—Listen	D—Do
GOAL: *I CAN* STATEMENTS	OBSERVE STUDENTS DOING:	LISTEN FOR STUDENTS SAYING:	DECIDE WHAT TO DO
• I can learn when I listen to others. • I can revise my thinking by listening to what others think of my work and by trying to understand their work.	• Sitting in circle meeting, eyes on the speaker, nodding, etc. (listening to an explanation of classmates and teacher) • Internalizing what has been said, processing it, and then acting upon it • Examining the shared work of others as represented on whiteboards, paper, etc. • Remaining open and nondefensive when receiving feedback from peers and teacher	• I heard her say that she put circles around the 5 sharpened pencils and counted the rest. • To find 87 – 53, I used the number line and counted from 53 to 60 for a jump of 7, from 60 to 80 for a jump of 10, and then from 80 to 87. I thought this was right until _____ asked me to look at all of my jumps again, and then I saw my mistake! • I think I understand what is right and what is wrong here. When adding 143 and 235, she added the hundreds and the ones correctly but made a mistake when she added 40 and 30 and got 60. • You're right: this is confusing now that I am hearing myself say it, so let me think about how to say this a different way.	• Ask *What questions do you have for _____?* *What do you agree with about her argument?* *What do you disagree with?* *What connections did you make as _____ was sharing?* *How can you make your argument stronger?* • Model how to give and receive feedback. • Explain the value of getting feedback. • Explain the value of giving feedback. • Underscore the importance of mistakes and learning from them. • Give ample wait time when asking for feedback; value the silence as thinking/processing time.

CLASSROOM LESSON: GET TO WORK

▶ The Inheritance

This problem has many variations and can be modified to fit various grade levels. This particular problem comes from the grade-five booklet called *Awesome Math Problems for Creative Thinking* (Greenes et al. 2000). It is definitely one you might like to try on your own before you see how students work to solve it. As you do, you will see how the problem calls MP2 into play, as it requires both abstract and quantitative reasoning. As you work through the problem and take some time to think about how you would organize your solution path so that others could follow it, provide evidence that supports your claims, and ready yourself to defend your thinking, you will see how MP3 is put to good use as well. Have fun with this one!

> Mrs. McGullicuddy left half of her estate to her son Sam.
> She left half of the remaining half to her cousin Fred.
> She left half of the remaining half to her nephew Horace.
> She left the remaining $25,000 for the care of her cat Chester.
> What was the total amount of Mrs. McGullicuddy's estate?

▶ Classroom Lesson Overview—Take a Look

- Grade: 5

- Focus Content Standard(s): 5.NF.2 Solve word problems involving addition and subtraction of fractions referring to the same whole, including cases of unlike denominators, e.g., by using visual fraction models or equations to represent the problem.

- Student Language: Solve word problem with fractions by using visual models and/or equations.

- Focus Math Practice: MP3: Construct Viable Arguments and Critique the Reasoning of Others

- I Can Statement: I can explain how and why my thinking makes sense.

- Lesson Setup:

The lesson began with three students reading aloud from the board: the Focus Content Standard in Student Language, the Focus Math Practice, and the I Can Statement.

Ms. Taylor started by asking what students knew about wills and testaments. A lively discussion ensued as students shared what they knew about why wills are made and what they might include. Ms. Taylor asked if any of the students had heard about people leaving money in their wills for their pets, and indeed, a few of them had. She told the students they would be solving a problem about a woman who had left money to several relatives as well as her cat, and that they would have to determine the total amount of her estate.

Ms. Taylor told the students that they would be responsible for assembling a trail of their reasoning in a way that supported their answers. She drew their attention back to the I Can statement and expanded on it, telling them that their explanations had to be convincing, credible, and viable, and that they would be sharing them with the class at the end of the lesson. When further prompted, the students said that they knew their explanations had to have words, numbers, and perhaps diagrams as well. They set off to work, excited to begin.

▶ Classroom Lesson Observations—Look Some More

It was clear that the students found this to be an intriguing problem, as there was a great deal of "buzzing" going on immediately. It was also interesting to note how some of the students instantly started to work on the problem with a partner, whereas some went off on their own to work individually. They all read and reread the problem aloud—several times—before they chose a strategy. The result was a variety of solution paths that were shared when Ms. Taylor pulled the students together later in the lesson. Judah explained, "Basically, I made a diagram of the whole thing. I split it in half for Sam first, and then I split the other half in half for Fred, and then the remaining quarter of it, I cut in half with one side for Horace and the other side for Chester. I knew that Chester got $25,000 and that's obviously the same as Horace. Together, those equal a quarter of the whole thing—$50,000—and Fred also got a quarter, so he got $50,000 by himself. That means the two quarters together are $25,000 plus $25,000 plus

$50,000, which equals 100,000. Obviously, this is the same for the other half of the whole, which means Sam got $100,000, and that means she left $200,000 in all." (See Figure 3.4 for Judah's work.)

Even though Judah did not write fractions in his written work, he used them to frame his thinking and then to justify his reasoning. Leon, on the other hand, went right to fractional notation to show how he solved the problem. He was able to show how he unpacked the problem both backward and forward, so to speak, by explaining that "Sam got ½ of the total, which also happens to equal ⁴⁄₈, Fred got ¼ and that equals ²⁄₈, and Horace got ⅛ and they all add to ⅞. Chester got $25,000 and that is ⅛ and now I can go backward to say that Horace got $25,000, and so on." (See Figure 3.5 for Leon's work.) Take a look at Shira's work (Figure 3.6) and notice how she methodically explained her reasoning, giving evidence to support how she got from one step to the next in her thinking.

CLASSROOM TEACHER REFLECTIONS — JESSICA TAYLOR, GRADE FIVE

▶ Lesson Reflection

I was thrilled to see how all of the students went to work on this problem right away. I was surprised that no one hesitated at the start and that they really did want to solve it. We have been working on that all year, and it was great to see.

I also loved that the kids solved the problem in so many different ways. Some worked backward right away and had no problem describing their thinking. It was nice to hear Jeremy when he said in such a matter-of-fact way, "Since you know the amount of money she gave in the end, you work backward from $25,000. Instead of dividing by 2, in the way the problem describes it, you multiply by 2 and then just keep doing it." I was blown away by his self-confidence in giving his argument.

I was also blown away when Judah was comparing his thinking with another student's and said that he really didn't use fractions "specifically." Shira, normally so shy, spoke right up and said that "Judah actually did use fractions" and that she knew that just by the way he divided his diagram and explained his

FIGURE 3.4

Judah's work on "The Inheritance" problem

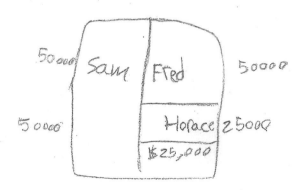

Judah **THE INHERITANCE**

I, Mrs. McGullicuddy, being of sound mind and body do hereby leave half of my estate to

Mrs. McGullicuddy left half of her estate to her son Sam.
She left half of the remaining half to her cousin Fred.
She left half of the remaining half to her nephew Horace.
She left the remaining $25,000 for the care of her cat Chester.

What was the total amount of Mrs. McGullicuddy's estate?

50000 | Sam | Fred | 50000
50000 | | Horace 25000
       | | $25,000

100000 – Sam
50000 – Fred
25000 – Horace
25000 – Chester
———————————
200,000

FIGURE 3.5

Leon's work on "The Inheritance" problem

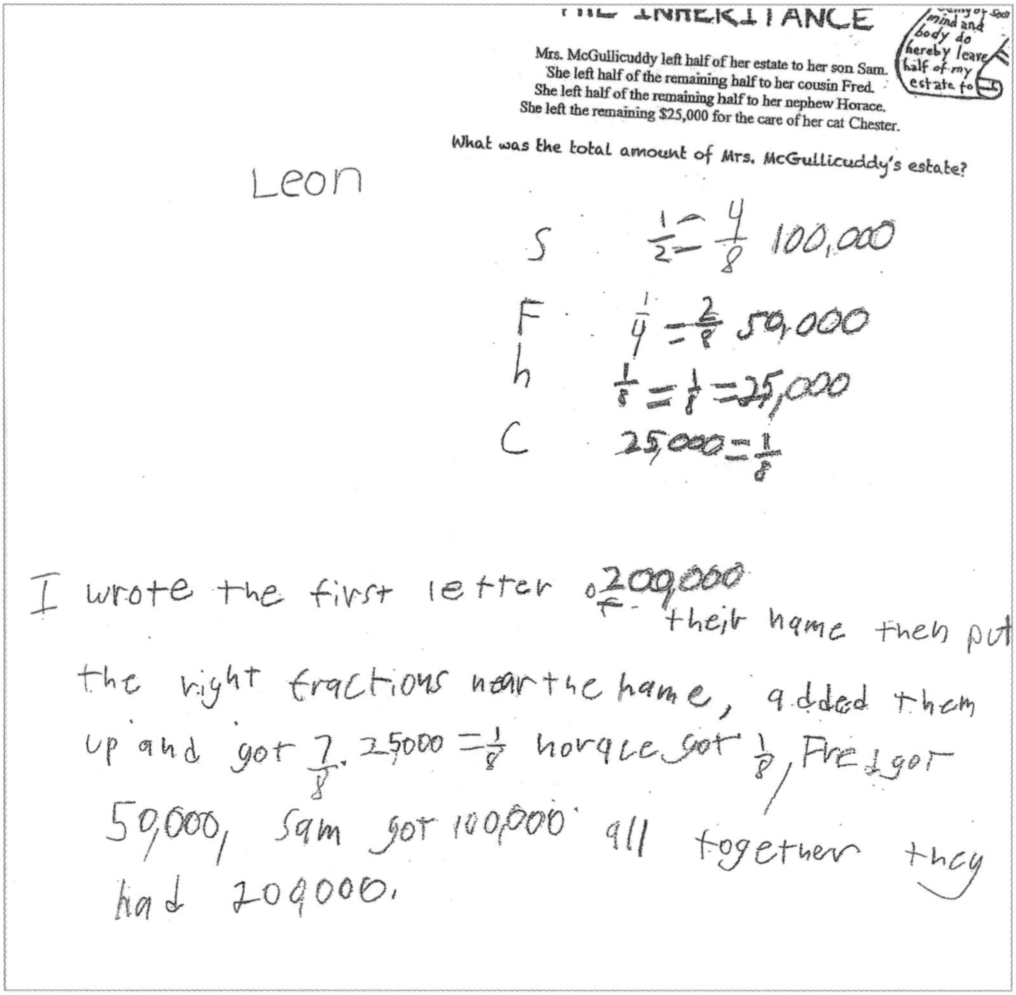

THE INHERITANCE

sound of mind and body do hereby leave half of my estate to

Mrs. McGullicuddy left half of her estate to her son Sam.
She left half of the remaining half to her cousin Fred.
She left half of the remaining half to her nephew Horace.
She left the remaining $25,000 for the care of her cat Chester.

What was the total amount of Mrs. McGullicuddy's estate?

Leon

S $\frac{1}{2} = \frac{4}{8}$ 100,000

F $\frac{1}{4} = \frac{2}{8}$ 50,000

h $\frac{1}{8} = \frac{1}{8} = 25,000$

C $25,000 = \frac{1}{8}$

I wrote the first letter of their name then put the right fractions near the name, added them up and got $\frac{7}{8}$. 25000 = $\frac{1}{8}$ horace got $\frac{1}{8}$, Fred got 50,000, Sam got 100,000 all together they had 200000.

thinking in words. I have been working hard this year to have the kids really listen to one another's explanations and find how they are both similar and different, and it seems as if some of this effort is paying off for them!

FIGURE 3.6

Shira's work on "The Inheritance" problem

Shira **THE INHERITANCE**

I, Mrs. McGullicuddy, being of sound mind and body do hereby leave half of my estate to

100,000 Mrs. McGullicuddy left half of her estate to her son Sam.
50,000 ¼ She left half of the remaining half to her cousin Fred.
She left half of the remaining half to her nephew Horace. ⅛
She left the remaining $25,000 for the care of her cat Chester. ⅛

What was the total amount of Mrs. McGullicuddy's estate?

$1,200,000

$$
\begin{array}{r}
25,000 \\
8 \\
\hline
\boxed{200,000}
\end{array}
$$

$$
\begin{array}{r}
50,000 \\
50,000 \\
\hline
100,000
\end{array}
$$

She left $\frac{1}{2}$ of her money to Sam.

She left $\frac{1}{2}$ of $\frac{1}{2}$ which is $\frac{1}{4}$ to Fred

She left $\frac{1}{2}$ of $\frac{1}{4}$ which is $\frac{1}{8}$ to Horace

She left what was left which is $\frac{1}{8}$ to her cat chester.

If 25,000 is $\frac{1}{8}$ of her money, you multiply 25,000 by 8 to get her total money which is

$200,000

▶ MP3 Reflection

I know that all of the Mathematical Practices are important, but I happen to think this is one of the most important. I see the ability to explain and defend your thinking as an essential life skill. I know that when I was in school, if I ever got asked about why I had solved a problem a certain way (which almost never happened, by the way), I assumed that it meant that I had the wrong answer, and I immediately questioned myself. My typical response was that I must have made a mistake and would try again. I think that this is the hardest part of this MP for me as a teacher. I constantly look for the right balance in my voice and my body language when I ask my students about how and why they solved a problem. I don't want them to feel threatened when asked to defend their thinking. I want them to see it as a positive step in their learning and that it is okay if they find an error in their thinking as they describe it to someone else. Actually, I want them to see that as a wonderful thing!

As I said in my reflection on "The Inheritance" lesson, I have also been working hard at having my students really and truly listen to each other. By the time they get to fifth grade, I think they should be able to find similarities and differences between how they and someone else solved a problem. This remains a top priority for me.

COMMENTS ABOUT MP3 FROM OTHER CLASSROOM TEACHERS

Kindergarten Teacher: I have loved watching this MP unfold in my kindergarten classroom. With so many ELL students in my class this year, language-building strategies have been blended into all areas of the curriculum, which is beneficial to all of my students. Watching my ELL students "turn and talk" and having them really do it, and hearing them defend their "arguments," is amazing. Though they sometimes mix up terms, they are learning how to defend themselves mathematically, and that's something I will continue to foster.

Grade Two Teacher: Helping students master this standard is *key* to making sure students *really* understand the problems they are solving. I think I have spent the most time on this standard, and it has taken most of the year for students to truly feel comfortable explaining and defending their strategies and challenging the thinking of others. By nature, students want to do what everyone else is doing. It takes a lot of math confidence to say, "I solved this problem by using base ten blocks" when other students are using mental math. By the end of the year, I was thrilled to see students solving problems in a variety of ways and discussing strategies.

COMMENTS ABOUT MP3 FROM STUDENTS

Ethan, Grade Two Student: It is important to explain your thinking, because when you go step-by-step, you might find a mistake. You can also help someone else so they don't fall behind.

Kevone, Grade Three Student: We do this Math Practice at Math Meeting when we go into partners and discuss our answers. We can help people answer tough questions.

Nathan, Grade Five Student: This is not always easy to do. Sometimes, I have to think very hard how to explain my thinking. I already know in my head what I have done, but it's kinda tricky to put that into words all the time so that someone who isn't in my head with me can see how I am thinking.

MATHEMATICAL PRACTICE 4:
MODEL WITH
MATHEMATICS

The purpose of models is not to fit the data but to sharpen the questions.

—SAMUEL KARLIN, AMERICAN MATHEMATICIAN

OVERVIEW

Although this MP certainly includes the use of objects, drawings, diagrams, concrete manipulatives, and more, it also moves beyond those parameters. An esteemed mathematics professor, Samuel Karlin, provided the short, pithy statement above that both encapsulates and embellishes the role of models. If questions are generated, and if they are sharp and precise, then modeling results in the application of these questions to make sense of the data and solve problems.

Mathematical Practice 4 is tightly interwoven with MPs 1, 2, 3, and 5. It activates both MP1 and 2, provides a foundation for MP3, and gives a kick to MP5. Modeling is used directly in solving problems, aids in thinking both abstractly and quantitatively, provides the core of a valid argument, and is a tool in and of itself. At the elementary level, this could look like students understanding what they are being asked to find in a problem, deciding how to represent the abstracted situation with tools such as counters or cubes, modeling it notationally with numbers and symbols, checking along the way to see if revisions to the model are needed, and then determining if the solution fits, and if it does not, revising the model again. Although elementary students may not actualize the highest level of mathematical modeling, the steps they are capable of making undergird their later development in this area.

GOALS

The three major goals of this Mathematical Practice focus on students being able to

1. understand that the "pure" mathematics they are learning can and should be used to solve problems in their everyday world both within and beyond the classroom walls;

2. use their mathematical knowledge to represent a more complex problem situation in a simpler way and then generalize back to the original problem;

3. access and use tools that can help them create models to analyze, represent, and map data, find relationships, and draw conclusions: among these are concrete objects, pictures, diagrams, charts, graphs, tables, expressions, equations, and formulas.

▶ Goal 1

To understand that the "pure" mathematics they are learning can and should be used to solve problems in their everyday world both within and beyond the classroom walls (Figure 4.1)

▶ Importance of This Goal

One way for students to see the value of the mathematics they are learning is to have them work with situations in their everyday lives that can be "mathematized." There are multiple sources for such problems (classroom textbooks, resource books, online sites, and so on), and many offer intriguing problems that move beyond a simple, formulaic solution. It is important, however, to ensure that these problems are relevant to your students; they need to see how some of what they have already learned can be applied to solving a problem they may actually face in the world beyond the classroom.

For this to happen, students must have experience with problems that are messy and do not fall into easy, pat pathways to a solution. For them to find these more complex solution pathways, students must have, in addition to procedural fluency, conceptual understanding so that they can identify

FIGURE 4.1
Goal 1

MATHEMATICAL PRACTICE 4: MODEL WITH MATHEMATICS

Goal 1: Understand that the "pure" mathematics they are learning can and should be used to solve problems in their everyday world both within and beyond the classroom walls

G—Goal	O—Observe	L—Listen	D—Do
GOAL: *I CAN* STATEMENTS	OBSERVE STUDENTS DOING:	LISTEN FOR STUDENTS SAYING:	DECIDE WHAT TO DO

• I can use math thinking in many places in my world.
 	
• I can see that the math we are learning can be used to help me think, wonder about, and make sense of my world.
	• Making connections between mathematics and "real life" situations both in and out of the classroom
	
	• Mucking and playing around with "messy" problems
	
	• Constructing a model to solve a problem and checking the resulting model for accurate alignment to the situation
	
	• Evaluating the effectiveness of a model
		• *To show the number and types of pets the kids in our class have, we could use a bar graph, fill in the information, and then check back to . . .*
		
		• *We have to plan a school garden where each class gets the same size plot. There's a lot to think about, like whether they have to be the same shape, whether they have to be in a certain order, and . . .*
		
		• *I'm not sure if this really matches what's going on in the problem—I think we have to find the sale price before we add the tax and then . . .*
		
		• *The PTO wants to know how much it will cost to get T-shirts for the school field day. We need to know how many kids, how many adults, if the cost is different for adults and kids and what about the custodian and the nurse, and . . .*
			• Ask:
			
			  Why did you think we are learning how to . . .?
			
			  Where do you see math being used?
			
			  How do you see math being used?
			
			  What are the important things (essential elements) in this problem?
			
			  What will help you decide how to solve this?
			
			• Discuss that understanding *modeling* as using concrete objects, pictorial representations (diagrams, tables, etc.), and abstract representations (numbers and symbols) is the beginning of what mathematical modeling is.
			
			• Provide "messy" problems—ones that move beyond rote application of skills and procedures and force students to meddle in and muck around with problems that cannot be solved instantaneously.
			
			• Present messy problems and have students decide what questions could be asked, given the situation.
			
			• Highlight that the goal of *modeling* is to make messy problems more clear mathematically.
			
			• Gather ideas for problems from the students by asking, *How could / did you use the math we have been learning at home? In the store? In the car?*
			
			• Make the connections between and among this MP with MPs 1, 2, 3, and 5.

models—"mental constructions" (Schoenfeld 1994)—that will allow them to begin to grapple with these types of problems. To manipulate these models, however, students must have experiences in which they have had to meld conceptual understanding with procedural knowledge, so they will avoid what John Tapper calls a student facing a "dichotomy between *knowing* the steps and *understanding* the steps" as something akin to "having a list of directions to get where you are going versus having a map of the entire area" (2012, 14).

▶ Goal 2

To use their mathematical knowledge to represent a more complex problem situation in a simpler way and then generalize back to the original problem (Figure 4.2)

▶ Importance of This Goal

Too often, students step back from a problem almost immediately because it seems "too hard" at first glance. This applies to all students, from the elementary students with whom I mostly work to the middle and high schoolers whom I tutor, as well as to those "below" and "above" grade level. I find that a fairly uncomplicated strategy—make it simpler—is not apparent enough in their problem-solving repertoire to be used as often as it could and should be. Students need to be taught explicitly a variety of ways to make a problem simpler. They need to see how, through modeling and practice, using smaller numbers and "friendly" numbers (whole numbers, multiples of ten, and so on) can allow them to solve the problem first with these simpler numbers and then apply the same strategies with the numbers in the original problem. They need modeling and practice in making a problem simpler by applying what they know to find out what they do not know. (For instance, they might not know the length of the entire trip, but they do know it was four times as far as the first leg of twenty-three miles, so by doubling twenty-three twice . . .) They need modeling and practice with identifying restrictions as aids in both making estimates and finding solutions. (The total can't be more than 100 percent because . . .) They need modeling and practice in seeing generalization as a way to make learning more accessible in that it gives them the chance to layer new learning onto prior knowledge. This may allow students to agree with Tapper, who says, "Generalization, it can be argued, is the goal of all learning. It means that students can

FIGURE 4.2
Goal 2

MATHEMATICAL PRACTICE 4: MODEL WITH MATHEMATICS

Goal 2: Use their mathematical knowledge to represent a more complex problem situation
in a simpler way and then generalize back to the original problem

G—Goal	O—Observe	L—Listen	D—Do
GOAL: *I CAN* STATEMENTS	OBSERVE STUDENTS DOING:	LISTEN FOR STUDENTS SAYING:	DECIDE WHAT TO DO
• I can make hard problems easier. • I can make hard problems simpler and then use those to help solve the harder ones.	• Using concrete objects to act out a problem • Making and using predictions and assumptions • Identifying what's known and what's unknown • Identifying variables, constants, and restrictions	• We have to cover this shape with trapezoids, but it will be easier to cover it first with hexagons and then double that. • He probably did not take any rests on his short walk to school, so the graph to match that would not come back to 0 for his speed. That means we can eliminate . . . • Let's start with what we know: The person got change and the clerk did not have any fives. She paid with a $50 bill, so we know the total spent had to be less than $50. We don't know the exact amount spent, so now we have to start there and then figure out two ways to give change without using fives. • We are looking for how much is left of a cake after one person eats ⅓ and then a second person eats ½. The first person ate ⅓ of the whole cake, so let's say that the second person ate ½ of what was left. There has to be less than ½ left, because we know . . .	• Ask: *What are you being asked to find or do in this problem?* *What might be a ballpark answer [estimate]? Why?* *What can't the answer be?* *What do you already know about this problem? What do you think you know?* *What don't you know?* *What would make this problem easier to solve?* • Be explicit about the role and purpose of both linguistic (for example, talking through a problem aloud) and nonlinguistic representations (such as drawing a picture) in getting to the root of a problem. • Model how using what you know can help in solving for something you do not yet know. • Stress the importance of making predictions, model how, and insist on having students make them. • Highlight how identifying restrictions (constraints, limits, controls) can help narrow the range of strategies and answers. • Provide opportunities for students to use "friendly" numbers (smaller, easier to work with) to make a more complex problem easier and then apply their solution path to the original problem.

use what they learn in class in a variety of new, unfamiliar circumstances. It is proof that students have incorporated new concepts and can use them—rather than learning them for the purpose of producing them for the teacher" (2012, 155).

▶ Goal 3

To access and use tools that can help them create models to analyze, represent, and map data, find relationships, and draw conclusions: among these are concrete objects, pictures, diagrams, charts, graphs, tables, expressions, equations, and formulas (Figure 4.3)

▶ Importance of This Goal

This component has obvious connections to MP5, Use Appropriate Tools Strategically. In this component, however, the focus is on using tools to create models that can lead to solving existing problems and to generating new questions that can lead to new problems. It is also through the use of these tools to construct models that students can be put into the position of determining if their models truly align with the problem, make sense in the context of the problem, and lead to a reasonable solution.

An additional benefit of this component is that students can see for themselves that a problem can be solved in multiple ways through the use of various models that use a variety of tools. Further, the sharing of models via the tools used can allow students to organize their thinking and lend credibility to their arguments (as in MP3). This sharing can promote constructive mathematical disagreements, as endorsed by Angela Barlow and Michael McCrory with the potential to "provide students with the impetus to think deeply about mathematics in an effort to make sense of a situation" as well as "to organize their thoughts, formulate arguments, consider other students' positions, and communicate their positions to their classmates" (2011, 531).

FIGURE 4.3
Goal 3

MATHEMATICAL PRACTICE 4: MODEL WITH MATHEMATICS

Goal 3: Access and use tools that can help them create models to analyze, represent, and map data, find relationships, and draw conclusions: among these are concrete objects, pictures, diagrams, charts, graphs, tables, expressions, equations, and formulas

G—Goal	O—Observe	L—Listen	D—Do
GOAL: *I CAN* STATEMENTS	OBSERVE STUDENTS DOING:	LISTEN FOR STUDENTS SAYING:	DECIDE WHAT TO DO
• I can use objects, pictures, numbers, and words to solve problems. • I can represent and then solve problems in more than one way, using objects, pictures, numbers, and words.	• Making sense of problems by using objects (for example, counters, ten frames, dominoes, and base ten blocks) • Making sense of problems using pictorial representations (such as number lines, diagrams, and tables) • Using the models to make sense of the mathematics being learned • Making connections and drawing conclusions from the models and asking new questions as a result	• I know that the girl in the problem ends up with 12 pencils and she starts with 5. I can use a full ten frame and 2 in another one to show 12, take out the 5 she started with, and then count what's left to get the answer. • I drew a picture of what is happening in the problem, and that makes it easier to see what math I need to do. • 24 ÷ 4 = 6 could mean 24 things arranged in 4 groups, and that means that the question has to be "How many in each group?" But it could mean that you start with 24 things and pull out 4 at a time, and that question would be different . . . • 2 × (4 + 2) = 12 could be shown as 4 girls—the red tiles—and 2 boys—the yellow tiles—in the cafeteria. The number of girls and boys doubles, so that's 8 red tiles plus 4 yellow tiles, which equals 12 kids in all. That's the same as adding 4 and 2, equaling 6, and then doubling to get 12. I wonder if this will work all the time.	• Ask: *Does your representation match the situation?* *How does your representation make the math clear?* *What do the results of the math tell you?* *Does the answer make sense?* *Does the answer give the information you want?* • Provide opportunities for students to learn to use multiple tools in applied ways. • Point out that some tools are better than others for certain problem situations. • Stress that most problems can be solved in multiple ways with different tools and representations by calling attention to various student solutions. • Underscore that using the tools is not the main goal—getting to and using the math is. • Provide messy problem situations and have the students generate possible questions.

CLASSROOM LESSON: GET TO WORK

▶ Show Me the Value: Base Ten

You may want to think about how you would present a problem of this sort to your students. The basic premise is for students to build with base ten blocks some sort of a structure that they see in their lives. There are, of course, limits and parameters that can be set so that the task can realistically be completed within one, perhaps two, classroom lessons. After students have built the structure, they are first asked to estimate its value and record their "ballpark" estimated answer. They then may have to write a description of it, determine its numerical value, and then, depending upon further variations, compare the value of their structures to others in the classroom. You may want to build a structure of your own in advance of reading the following sections and anticipate how your students might go about solving the problem.

As is the case with most problems, this one integrates multiple Mathematical Practices into the work it takes to solve it. It requires students to meld abstract and quantitative reasoning (MP2) with using a mathematical tool (MP5), along with a level of requisite precision (MP6). Additionally and perhaps more central to the task, each student will be drawing from the real world, creating a model of it, and then analyzing that model and drawing conclusions—components of MP4.

▶ Classroom Lesson Overview—Take a Look

- Grade: 2

- Focus Content Standard(s): 2.NBT.1 Understand that the three digits of a three-digit number represent amounts of hundreds, tens, and ones; 2.NBT.3 Read and write numbers to 1000 using base ten numerals, number names, and expanded form; 2.NBT.4 Compare two three-digit numbers based on meanings of the hundreds, tens, and ones digits; 2.NBT.7 Add and subtract within 1000, using concrete models or drawings and strategies based on place value, properties of operations

- Student Language: Find and compare the value of concrete representations by using place-value models.

- Focus Math Practice: MP4: Model with Mathematics

- I Can Statement: I can represent and solve problems using objects, pictures, numbers, and words.

- Lesson Setup:

Mrs. Freud, the classroom teacher, called on three students to read aloud from the board the Focus Content Standard in Student Language, the Focus Math Practice, and the I Can Statement. She then kicked off the lesson by asking, "When do we use math in our everyday lives?" and followed up with a brief discussion of how and why math is of value to all. The students talked about how they use math at home, at the store, in their sports, and so on.

Mrs. Freud continued with the setup by asking the students, "Can you think of a 'structure,' something you see or use, and then think about how you could show—represent—it with base ten blocks?" She explained that they would each make their own structure and had to use some units (1s), some longs or rods (10s), and some flats (100s). Mrs. Freud did suggest that they not build "up" too much, to prevent the "crumbling" of buildings. The students were instructed that they had to describe their structure with words and pictures. They were also told to make an estimate of the "base ten value" of their construction, write it in colored marker or pencil, and "ring" it to identify it as the "ballpark"/estimated answer. All students were told they would each then determine the actual value and record how they found it, showing their thinking.

Students were directed to their group settings, with some groups of two, some of three, and one of four. Mrs. Freud further differentiated the task by having some students find a structure with a value that was greater than theirs and one that was less, find the difference between theirs and the other structures, and then explain how they determined the differences.

▶ Classroom Lesson Observations—Look Some More

The students couldn't wait to start this task. They knew that they had to get to it, since Mrs. Freud had told them they would have eight to ten minutes to do their building. There were collections of base ten blocks at each of the group settings, so they dug right in and started to build. Mrs. Freud checked in on students as they worked: "Tell me about your structure so far. What does your mental image of it look like? How are you planning to build it? What might be an estimate/ballpark of the value? What would be a value that would be way too high/low for what you've built so far?"

The engagement in this task was clearly evident in the way the students attended to their building. They could be heard describing aloud to a classmate what they were building and how they planned to do it. This helped when it came time for each to write a description. The level of details in the written descriptions varied, with some more extensive than others.

Estimating the value of the structures was relatively easy for some students. Amaiyah looked at her "mousetrap" (see Figure 4.4 for Amaiyah's work) and said, "I know it is more than 100, but I think it is less than 200, so I'm guessing in the middle." She wrote her estimate, put a ring around it, and left it alone, as did Aaron (see Figure 4.5 for Aaron's work). Mia, on the other hand, changed her estimate a few times because "it isn't right." (See Figure 4.6 for Mia's work.) Although some of the students made ballpark estimates of "friendly" numbers (multiples of ten, for example), more precise numbers were recorded for the estimate. Many students had a hard time with the idea of an estimate, thinking that it was more important to be "exact," they told Mrs. Freud.

As students worked to find the exact value of the structures, it was clear that some were quite organized in their approach. Aaron separated the blocks, wrote what they were, recorded the value of each type, and then added the partial sums from the largest to the smallest to find the total. Amaiyah had a similar approach but showed the partial values on the number line to find her total. Many students were not as organized in their counting and benefited from Mrs. Freud's guiding questions: "How many flats do you have? What would be a good next step now? What tool could help you find the total?"

FIGURE 4.4

Amaiyah's work on the "Show Me the Value" problem

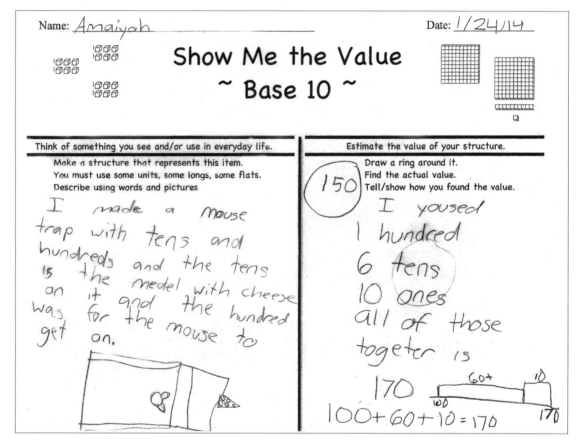

CLASSROOM TEACHER REFLECTIONS —
NANCY FREUD, GRADE TWO

▶ Lesson Reflection

When we first did this lesson, the students were just becoming familiar with the MPs and had not yet learned three-digit addition and subtraction. Building the structures was not a problem, but finding the value was challenging for many

FIGURE 4.5

Aaron's work on the "Show Me the Value" problem

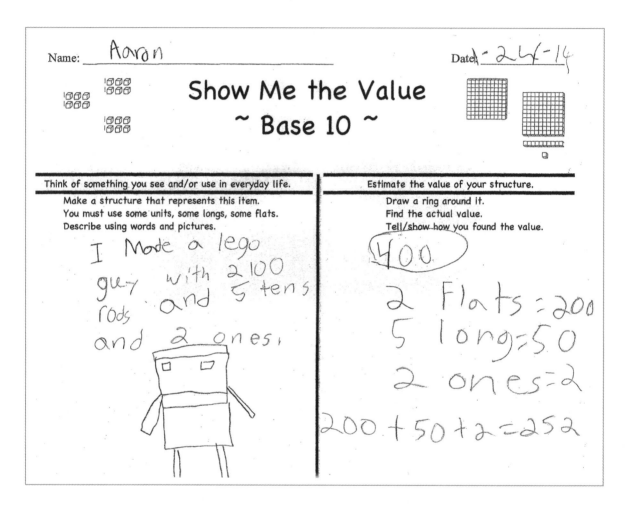

of them. They did not have an organized approach to counting their base ten blocks, and some of them were recounting blocks that had already been counted. Even so, everyone was able to come up with a total value (some correct, some not). The biggest roadblock was finding the difference between their structure and a partner's, since they had learned only two-digit subtraction at this point. I

FIGURE 4.6

Mia's work on the "Show Me the Value" problem

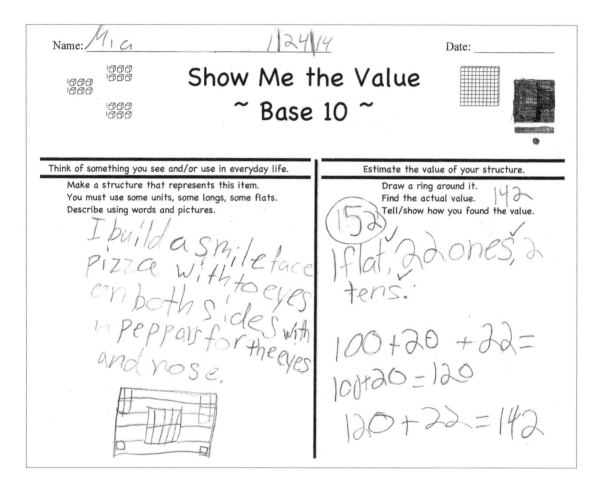

was interested to see how they would tackle this. As expected, some persevered, some guessed, and some just gave up.

I decided to do the lesson again later in the year. By this time, the students were much more aware of the MPs. Further, they had worked more with three-digit addition and subtraction. There was quite a difference both in how they found the total value and in how they found the differences between structures. Aaron, for example, had just compared the actual base ten blocks

FIGURE 4.7

Aaron's follow-up work

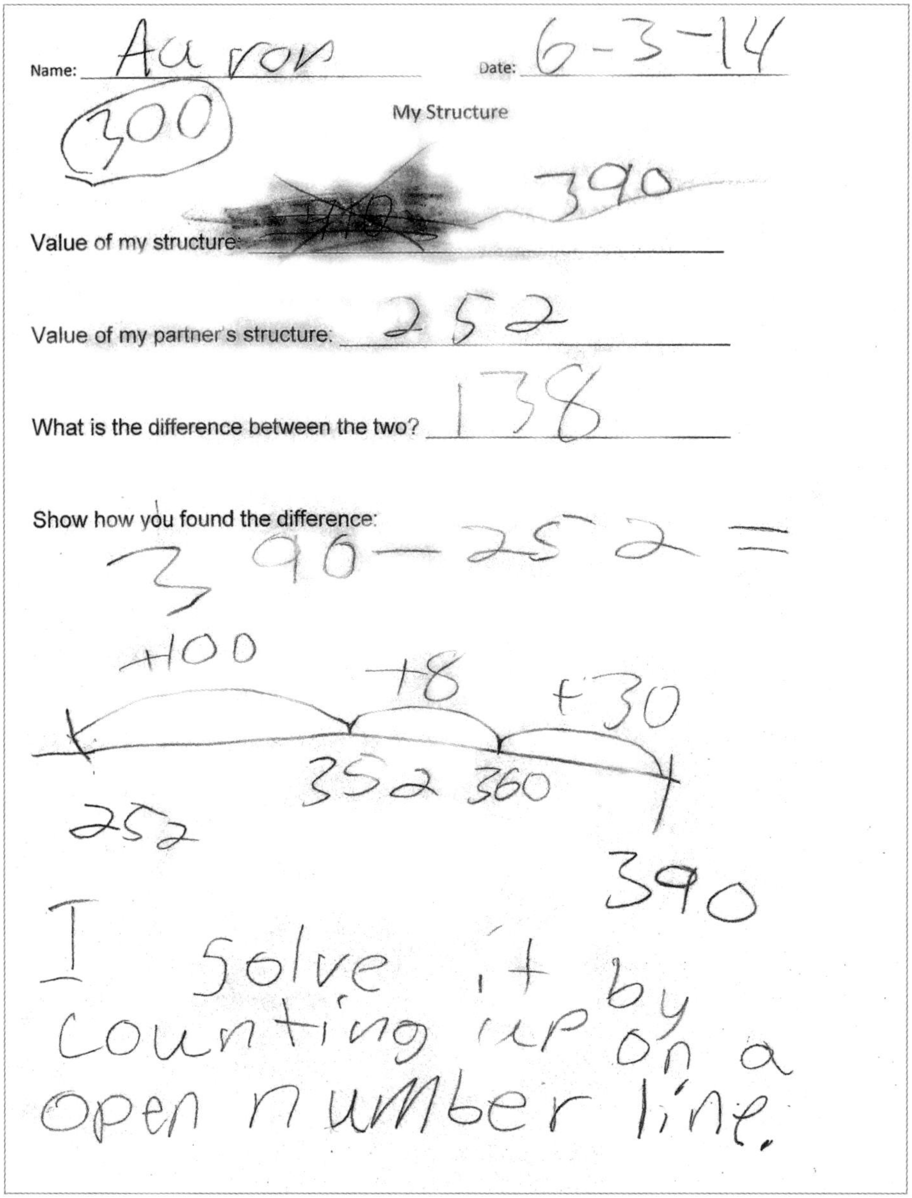

Name: _Aaron_   Date: _6-3-14_

(300)   My Structure

390

Value of my structure: _____

Value of my partner's structure: _252_

What is the difference between the two? _138_

Show how you found the difference:

$$390 - 252 =$$

+100   +8   +30

252   352 360   390

I solve it by counting up on a open number line.

FIGURE 4.8

Davia's follow-up work

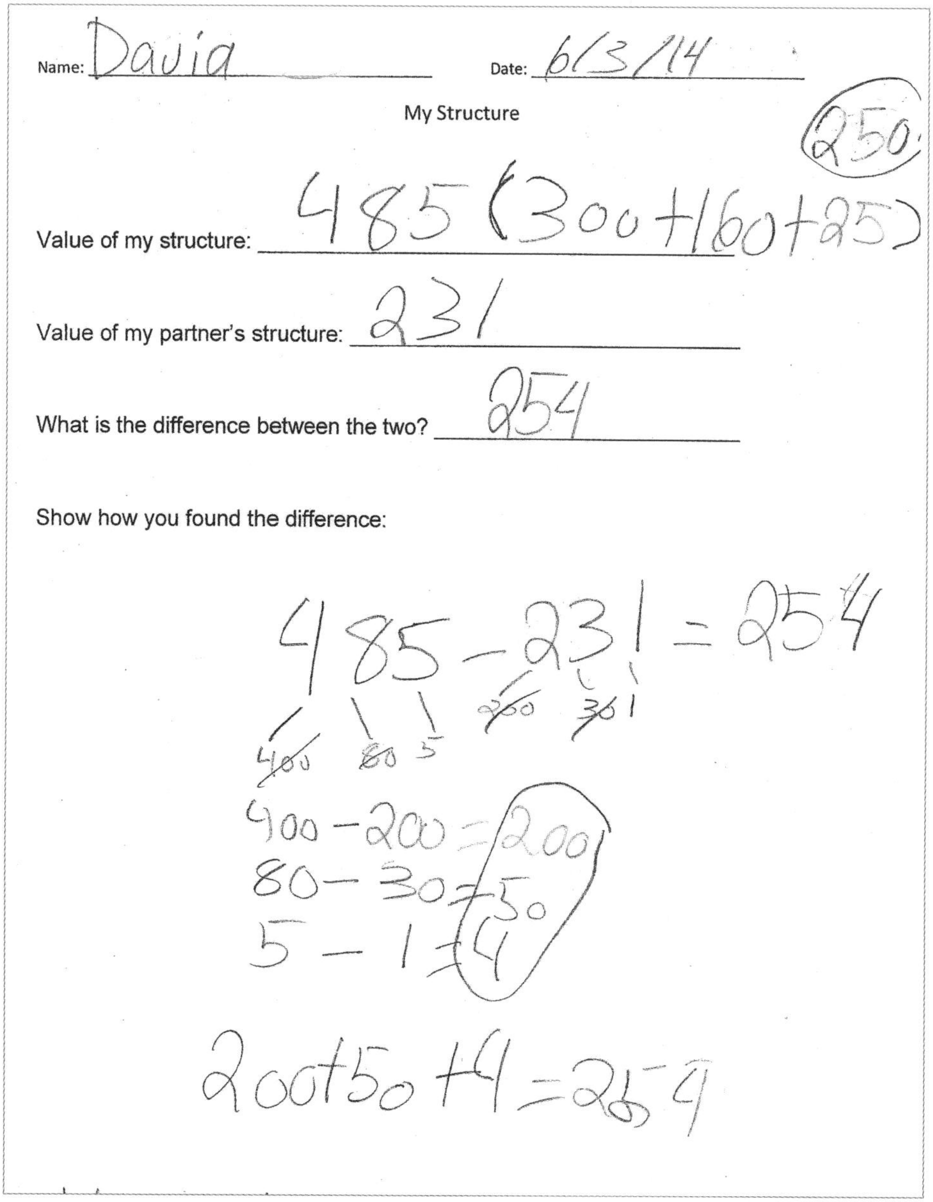

Name: Davia   Date: 6/3/14

My Structure

(250)

Value of my structure: $485 \ (300+160+25)$

Value of my partner's structure: 231

What is the difference between the two?   254

Show how you found the difference:

$$485 - 231 = 254$$

$400 \quad 80 \quad 5 \qquad 200 \quad 301$

$$900 - 200 = 200$$
$$80 - 30 = 50$$
$$5 - 1 = 4$$

$$200 + 50 + 4 = 254$$

and counted the remaining difference between the two. The second time around, Aaron used an open number line (see Figure 4.7). Davia, who had experienced difficulty with this the first time the lesson was done, was much more confident in her approach and did a great job explaining her thinking (see Figure 4.8 for Davia's work).

I expected to see correct calculations, but what I didn't expect to see was how the MPs had completely changed their approach to solving this problem. Overall, the atmosphere in the room was productive. Yes, they had fun building the structures, but they were more interested in getting to the "meat" of the problem. When counting the value of their structure, they dismantled it, grouped the hundreds, tens, and ones, and counted in an organized fashion (MP5). They worked with their partners in a respectful way, explaining their thinking and discussing strategies (MP3). When asked, they could explain their strategy in a meaningful way. I was most struck by one group of boys: Matthew was having trouble calculating the value of his structure. Ethan offered to help and showed Matthew how to count it. Colin, checking for precision (MP6), recounted the structure and got a value that was different from Ethan's. Rather than argue over who was correct, which would have happened at the beginning of the year, the three of them calmly counted and recounted until they all got the same value (MP1). They had used models to further their thinking and to find relationships (MP4). My students had become mathematical thinkers who were interested in more than just getting "an answer."

▶ MP4 Reflection

This particular Mathematical Practice sounds and looks somewhat easy at first, but it is not. The more I work with this one, the more I realize that it is harder than it looks. Before I started really working with the MPs in general, I knew almost nothing about any of them. They were all basically a bunch of jargon to me. I had no idea how they fit in with the Common Core, nor did I have any idea about how I was going to translate all this technical math language and make it accessible to second graders.

Model with Mathematics initially seemed pretty straightforward to me. It was when I began to dissect it and try to get at what it is all about that I started to grasp a better idea of it. I understand that it moves beyond just using manipulatives and drawings, diagrams, and tables to explain how you have solved a problem. I understand that it is connected to using and applying mathematical thinking and mathematical tools to make connections, to make predictions about real situations. Because I consider myself a reflective practitioner, I am always thinking of ways to improve my instruction. I will continue to grapple with how to bring this MP as well as all the others to my second graders.

COMMENTS ABOUT MP4 FROM OTHER CLASSROOM TEACHERS

Grade One Teacher: At this level of development, I think this Mathematical Practice is all about, or mostly about, having students work at making sense of and dealing with "real-world" problems and using a variety of tools to solve them. That term—*real-world*—makes me stop and think. For my level, I am interpreting this as not doing problems about unicorns and talking pumpkins, but letting my students see how problems about how many people can sit at a table, how long it takes to get to the store, and how many lunch boxes will fit in the bucket are the kinds of things they need to be exposed to and have opportunities to think about in real ways. This MP is a definite work in progress for me.

Grade Four Teacher: Making sense of math in the world and using math "things" to do it: this is what I now think MP4 is about at my level. I used to think that it was only about using manipulatives to solve problems—to "model" what was done with the base ten blocks or cubes, and so on that were involved in finding the answer. I am beginning to see that this MP has more to it and that it grows more sophisticated as the students grow. I have to admit the term *mathematical modeling* intimidates me. I was a good memorizer and did okay in math through school, but I do not consider myself a strong mathematical thinker. I do know that if I hope to support my students in developing this MP and all the others as well, I am going to have "model" how to use mathematical models, so I've got some work to do.

COMMENTS ABOUT MP4 FROM STUDENTS

Joel, Kindergarten Student: We use our fingers all the time to model like I did for this problem. I am showing three kids who were at the table on this hand and then the two kids who came over on my other hand, and then I can put them together.

Tamika, Grade Two Student: This is all about using things to help you figure out things about things that are in our world.

Jaylisse, Grade Four Student: There are a lot of things you can use to work on real problems. The base ten blocks can be used to work with place value and can help by giving you a visual model of what you are doing.

MATHEMATICAL PRACTICE 5:
USE APPROPRIATE TOOLS STRATEGICALLY

The expectations of life depend upon diligence; the mechanic that would perfect his work must first sharpen his tools.

—CONFUCIUS

OVERVIEW

Each of the four words of this Mathematical Practice is important to consider. Let's start with tools. In a general sense, a tool is something that is used to do a job, complete a task, or reach a goal. For a tool to be useful, however, it must be the right tool—the appropriate one—for the task at hand. It almost goes without saying that for a tool to be helpful, it must be brought into play, operated, used. More important, it must be used in a deliberate, intentional, purposeful way—strategically. Confucius had it right. If I may paraphrase, for any worker to be successful in his work, he must "sharpen" his tools and then use them well, thoughtfully, and consistently—with "diligence."

So what does this mean in terms of supporting students in choosing and using the right tools in the right way at the right time? First, it means having all sorts of mathematical tools available and accessible, from pencils and rulers to calculators and computer applications, to aid in both mental and written mathematics. Further, it means that students must know how to use these tools correctly: someone needs to model and/or teach the students explicitly how and when to use them. Additionally, it means that students must have opportunities to see others make decisions and to make their own decisions about which tool might be a good one to use and the right time to use it.

I've found a "backpack of tools"—a collection of tools at students' disposal—to be very useful. As a classroom teacher, I started the school year by bringing an empty backpack into the classroom and putting it on one of my students. (Some years I would swap the backpack for an empty toolbox.) I would tell them that even though this particular backpack was empty, I knew that they were coming into this year with many tools already in their mathematical backpacks in terms of knowledge and skills. I told them they would be adding to their backpacks throughout the year, including new tools to help them become stronger mathematical thinkers. As the year progressed, we would add both physical and symbolic representations of new tools (base ten blocks, a ten frame, a diagram showing a new mental math strategy, and so on) that would help in mathematical thinking and problem solving, adding to their ever-growing repertoires.

GOALS

The three major goals of this Mathematical Practice focus on students being able to

1. develop familiarity with and understand the purpose of tools in problem solving while recognizing both their power and their limitations;

2. make sound decisions about when (and when not) to use tools and then select the tools that best fit problem situations; and

3. use classroom tools and external resources to deepen mathematical thinking, forge connections, and as springboards to mathematical "pondering."

▶ Goal 1

To develop familiarity with and understand the purpose of tools in problem solving while recognizing both their power and their limitations (Figure 5.1)

▶ Importance of This Goal

It may seem obvious, but if students are not familiar with a tool, they are most likely going to have difficulty using it appropriately and strategically. Many of us often introduce students to various tools by demonstrating their use in whole-class and/or small-group lessons. It is important that while doing this, you think aloud as you use the tools, show how you are manipulating them, and explicitly explain your actions. Even more important, however, is for students to move beyond being spectators and get their hands "dirty," touching, feeling, and manipulating the tools for themselves.

FIGURE 5.1

Goal 1

MATHEMATICAL PRACTICE 5: USE APPROPRIATE TOOLS STRATEGICALLY

Goal 1: Develop familiarity with and understand the purpose of tools in problem solving while recognizing both their power and their limitations

G—Goal	O—Observe	L—Listen	D—Do
GOAL: *I CAN* STATEMENTS	OBSERVE STUDENTS DOING:	LISTEN FOR STUDENTS SAYING:	DECIDE WHAT TO DO

• I can use tools to help me understand and solve problems.
 	
• I can see how using tools can help in solving problems, and I know how to choose and use them well.
	• Accessing tools (eventually without prompting)
	
	• Using a variety of tools that include the following and are developmentally appropriate:
	mental math
	paper/pencil (diagrams, etc.)
	blocks: attribute
	            base ten
	            geo
	            pattern
	            tangrams
	counters: assorted
	            two-color
	cubes: linking
	            number
	            centimeter
	            inch
	clocks (grades one to three)
	hundreds chart/ two-hundreds chart/ three-hundreds chart
	square-inch tiles
	ten frames
	fraction: bars
	           circles
	measuring: beaker
	           cylinders
	           meter stick
	           ruler (in/cm)
	           springscale
	           tape
	           yardstick
	calculators
	computers
		• I think the answer will be more than 50 because there are already 5 full ten frames and there are some extras.
		
		• I know the answer is wrong because I estimated it should be between 140 and 150, and if you look on the 200 grid, you can see that you took away one too many tens, which made your answer in the 130s.
		
		• We can make a bar graph to show the favorite ice cream flavors, and then we can compare to see which is the favorite of the whole school.
		
		• This would make much more sense if we used the tiles to show the different rectangles. Then we can compare and go from there.
			• Ask:
			What tool might help you with this problem?
			What other tools might also help?
			How can this tool help?
			Why did you choose this tool?
			What tools in your "toolbox" are your favorites? Why?
			
			• Make tools accessible and visible; have them in clear and labeled containers in an identified place, organized and ready for use.
			
			• Provide specific tools for certain lessons (have them in containers in group settings, etc.), but remind students that additional tools are still available to them.
			
			• Present new tools with explicit instructions for their use, as well as an overview of their purposes and their limitations.
			
			• Allow time for students to "mess around" with new tools to gain familiarity with them.
			
			• Remind students that the tools don't give them the answers—they help them find the answers.

We tend to think of tools, especially in the younger grades, primarily as concrete manipulatives, such as counters, tiles, base ten blocks, calculators, rulers, and so on. These serve younger children well, but they also are useful in upper grades. Students need to be exposed to many types of tools, in addition to concrete ones. Pictorial and symbolic representations that include tables, diagrams, and graphic organizers such as Venn diagrams, flowcharts, and word-association banks are wonderful tools to help organize all types of thinking. They offer entry into many mathematical problems. Exposing students to a variety of tools and letting them use them to explore can open the doors to problem solving even wider. Because students learn differently and a problem can often be solved with more than one tool, having a variety of tools that students are familiar with "may make the difference with regard to whether a problem is accessible" (Dacey, Lynch, and Salemi 2013, 117).

When students see firsthand how mathematical tools can help them—when they see how a ten frame can help them count, how a number line can help them compute, how tangrams can help them visualize and play around spatially—they understand how the tools increase their power to think mathematically. The flip side is that students also need to see that tools are limited in what they can help them do. For instance, square-inch tiles have many uses, but they are not much help in finding the volume of a cylinder. This leads into the next goal of this MP.

▶ Goal 2

To make sound decisions about when (and when not) to use tools and then select the tools that best fit problem situations (Figure 5.2)

▶ Importance of This Goal

Just because a tool can do certain things and we enjoy using it does not mean that it is the right one for a particular job. Yes, a calculator can provide an exact answer to a computation, but the problem may call only for an estimate, and mental math is better suited to that. Yes, we have fun using the retractable measuring tape, but is it the right tool for finding the area of a pattern block drawing? Students need ample opportunities to make decisions about a variety of ways to use tools. First, however, they need to determine if a concrete or pictorial tool is needed or not; they sometimes need to be reminded that their mental math strategies are powerful enough to do the job! If the problem calls

FIGURE 5.2
Goal 2

MATHEMATICAL PRACTICE 5:
USE APPROPRIATE TOOLS STRATEGICALLY

Goal 2: Make sound decisions about when (and when not) to use tools
and then select the tools that best fit problem situations

G—Goal	O—Observe	L—Listen	D—Do
GOAL: *I CAN* STATEMENTS	OBSERVE STUDENTS DOING:	LISTEN FOR STUDENTS SAYING:	DECIDE WHAT TO DO

• I can choose "just-right" tools.
 	
• I can decide when a tool is needed and then choose the right tool to match the situation.
	• Using mental math and paper and pencil to solve problems
	
	• Making use of tools already provided as well as accessing tools on their own
	
	• Making conscious decisions about whether or not a tool is needed
	
	• Selecting which level of tool is needed and choosing a tool that matches the problem context
		• I can see the domino patterns in my head and count them to find how many in all.
		
		• The graph tells how many people like each flavor. Then if I write the number sentence and use a hundreds chart, I can solve the problem.
		
		• Using a yardstick will make this easier than using a ruler.
		
		• Using the calculator will help us test these divisibility rules for larger numbers more easily.
			• Ask
			
			  Why did you choose to solve this problem using . . . ?
			
			  Can this be solved with a different tool?
			
			  Is one tool better than another for this problem? Why?
			
			  In what kinds of problems would it be helpful to use . . . ?
			
			  What tool could help someone see [visualize] the problem?
			
			• Underscore that tools are not "crutches" and are used by all mathematicians.
			
			• Insist that students give or record a "ballpark" answer—an estimate—before they begin to work on a problem, and then have them later check their answer against it.
			
			• Ask what, if any, tools will help them find the answer.
			
			• Model how to determine which tools would be better or best, asking, Can this be solved mentally, with paper or pencil, or with some other tool?
			
			• Engage students in discussions about how most problems can be solved with more than one tool, and have them share the various ways different tools led to solutions.

for something other than mental math, however, they then need to decide which tool or tools could be used to solve that problem. Further, students need to experience changing their minds about their choice if the selected tool is not helpful and another tool would be a better option.

Asking students questions about how they decided to use a specific tool is a good place to start. Then as they are using a tool, it makes sense to ask them how they think it is working; they should be able to justify why the tool they chose is a good one. After they have completed the task at hand, students should be able to evaluate how effective the tool was in helping with the mathematics. Did it really help, and if so, how? In *Common Core Mathematics in a PLC at Work*, the authors make a great point to this end: "If students use tools to engage in mathematics and walk away from the experience with little or no understanding of the mathematics, then the use of the tools was ineffective" (Kanold 2012, 46).

▶ Goal 3

To use classroom tools and external resources to deepen mathematical thinking, forge connections, and as springboards to mathematical "pondering" (Figure 5.3)

▶ Importance of This Goal

Simply put, "An excellent mathematics program integrates the use of mathematical tools and technology as essential resources to help students learn and make sense of mathematical ideas, reason mathematically, and communicate their mathematical thinking" (NCTM 2014, 78). I couldn't agree more—especially with the "essential" part—and have seen the way in which tools can and do help students dig into the mathematics that underlies what they are doing in math. Using concrete manipulatives such as counters, cubes, and base ten blocks can helps students "see" what is happening as they add or subtract. As a result, they move beyond procedural understanding to bulk it up and weigh it down with conceptual understanding, allowing them to make connections between the actions of joining together and taking away, for example. Using cubes or tiles to make a 4-by-5 array and a 5-by-4 array can help students see and understand the commutative property of multiplication. Geoboards and pattern blocks can help promote visualization skills and foster the development of spatial thinking, again providing opportunities for students

FIGURE 5.3
Goal 3

MATHEMATICAL PRACTICE 5:
USE APPROPRIATE TOOLS STRATEGICALLY

Goal 3: Use classroom tools and external resources to deepen mathematical thinking, forge connections, and as springboards to mathematical "pondering"

G—Goal	O—Observe	L—Listen	D—Do
GOAL: *I CAN* STATEMENTS	OBSERVE STUDENTS DOING:	LISTEN FOR STUDENTS SAYING:	DECIDE WHAT TO DO
• I can use many tools to help me think as a mathematician. • I can use tools to explore mathematical ideas and advance my thinking.	• Using the hundreds chart to explore our number system • Comparing and contrasting shapes when using pattern blocks, geoblocks, etc. • Using a calculator to explore properties of operations • Accessing data from multiple sources (such as people, print materials, and online resources)	• If it goes in jumps of 10, like 49 to 59 to 69 to 79, then 89 and 99, it should be 109, right? • I can make groups of shapes with attribute blocks in many ways. I wonder how many ways I can sort pattern blocks. • I know that the order does not matter in addition and multiplication. Does it matter in subtraction and division? • I know that 8×7 is 56. If I double 8 and double 7, will the answer be double 56? Why or why not?	• Ask *What can you explore with the calculator, this program, this . . . ?* *If you could invent a mathematical tool, what would you want it to do?* *When is it better or more efficient to use mental math or paper and pencil than to use a tool?* *What did this tool help you learn?* *What connections did you make as you used this tool?* • Be aware that not every student has access to the same kinds of resources outside the classroom. • Explore ways to work with parents, parent organizations, and outside funding sources to provide access to appropriate high-tech tools for all students. • Discuss with students that just because a tool is new and glitzy, it does not replace mental math and other such tools. • Provide problems for students to engage in that are provocative and push them to want to explore. • Allow time for students to ask provocative questions of their own, to share what they have been exploring, what other questions came about as a result, etc.

to make connections and "see" mathematical relationships with greater clarity. Calculators can open the door to explorations with numbers, helping students investigate numerical patterns and make discoveries that may have been obscured from them. Computers, smartphones, and tablets can be used in multiple ways that promote exploration and understanding, from gathering data to providing multiple representations of that data, presenting opportunities to connect with other schools across the country and around the world as students seek answers to questions that stem from their classroom work as well as ones they have generated themselves.

I love the word *ponder* and all that it can mean. It holds within it the promise of new thinking, of productive imagining, of inspired connectivity. The use of tools in mathematics can support such pondering on the parts of our students and makes it easier for them to pose questions, to run with their curiosity, to imagine. One of my favorite quotes is one that is often attributed to Albert Einstein (although there is some skepticism about whether he actually said it). Regardless of its origin, it connects in a substantive way to this MP: "Logic will get you from A to B. Imagination will take you everywhere." I see the appropriate use of mathematical tools as an effective vehicle for taking our students to previously unattainable mathematical places.

CLASSROOM LESSON—GET TO WORK

▶ Let It Snow

The focus problem for this MP revolved around a wonderful book by Rebecca Bond, *This Place in the Snow* (2004) that tells the story of what happens when a small town awakens to a blanket of sparkling, glittering, glistening snow. At one point, the children, adults, and some animals are gathered together, mesmerized as the snowplow does its work and the mound of snow grows and grows into a beautiful mountain. Although the story could generate many mathematical questions, the one presented to the students was about the number of people and animals present. Some students also worked to find the total number of footprints in the snow.

▶ Classroom Lesson Overview—Take a Look

- Grade: K

- Focus Content Standard(s): K.CC.5 Count to answer "how many?" questions about as many as 20 things arranged in a line; K.CC.6 Identify whether the number of objects in one group is greater than, less than, or equal to the number of objects in another group; K.OA.1 Represent addition with objects.

- Student Language: Count to find out how many, to compare, to add

- Focus Math Practice: MP5: Use appropriate tools strategically

- I Can Statement: I can use tools to help me understand and solve problems.

- Lesson Setup:

Mrs. Lanier began by telling the students as they gathered at the rug that today they would be hearing a story first and then doing some math that related to the story. She pointed to and read the Focus Content Standard in Student Language, the Focus Math Practice, and the I Can statement.

Mrs. Lanier read the story aloud to the students and then asked where in the story the students saw math. The discussion segued into the importance of counting in everyday life, as well as how often addition is used to find the answers to questions.

Mrs. Lanier asked the students about different ways they might add and which tools from their "toolboxes" could help. The general consensus was that counters and ten frames would work well for most of them. Mrs. Lanier asked why this was the case. Halysabell said, "You can see the answers on the ten frames as you do the work." Mrs. Lanier then asked how students could know whether there is more of one thing than another and how they could find the answer to that type of question.

Mrs. Lanier placed students into partner groups and then set them to work to find the answers to the questions on the recording sheet. (She had also predetermined differentiations and made them accordingly.)

▶ Classroom Lesson Observations—Look Some More

All of the students were immediately captivated by the story. It was January, it had just snowed, and they were laser focused, full of predictions about what their math work would be. When they were sent off to find the answers, they all went with purpose and excitement.

The students knew that the various workstations set around the room housed both tools for them to use and a copy of the book's illustration for them to refer to as they worked. Most chose to use the foam ten frames; one student plugged one peg into each hole of the frame as the other student touched each person and animal in the illustration, demonstrating a one-to-one correspondence.

All of the groups were successful in determining that there were twelve people and three animals in the snow. Because they were familiar with ten frames, the students filled them in an organized and deliberate way. Kayla filled in the worksheet with dark circles for each person and animal, wrote 12 and 3 in the appropriate places, and then filled in one more circle to show the answers for one more (both correct even though she reversed the digits in 13). (See Figure 5.4 for Kayla's work.) As for the question of whether there were more animals or people, she knew that there were more people but could not say how many more. She provided more information, however, when she wrote that 12 is "bigr," and when asked how she knew that, she replied, "I knowed it because it's on the number line like that." Paula also could not determine how many more but wrote that "3 is les 12." When asked what she wrote and how she knew this, she said, "Three is less than twelve, and all you have to do is look at my ten frames and you can see it for yourself!" (See Figure 5.5 for Paula's work.) Jonathan used the ten frames to show the twelve people but "just saw with my eyes that there are three animals." Although he knew that there were more people than animals, the question he answered was different from the one asked about the difference between the two, and he used a different tool—counters—to find the total of animals and people. (See Figure 5.6 for Jonathan's work.)

Eyram used a variety of tools—tallies, ten frames, counters, and fingers—in his work. He used the ten frames to show the number of people and animals. To find the difference between people and animals, he made tally marks for each and "circled three of the people to go with the three animals and then counted what was left to figure it out." (See Figure 5.7 for Eyram's first page of work.) He was then ready to find the number of footprints. He said, "We should count by twos the tallies for the people to find all the people feet." From there, using his fingers, he said, "The animals have 4 feet, and 4 plus 4 plus 4 make 12."

FIGURE 5.4

Kayla's work on the "Let It Snow" problem

Name: Kayla   Date: 1/16/14

Let It Snow

~ There are ___12___ people in the snow.

~ This is how I know.

~ 1 more = 31

~ There are 3 animals in the snow.

~ This is how I know.

~ 1 more = 4

~ There are more

animals   (people)

~ There are 12 5 6 more
of them and this is how I know.

FIGURE 5.5

Paula's work on the "Let It Snow" problem

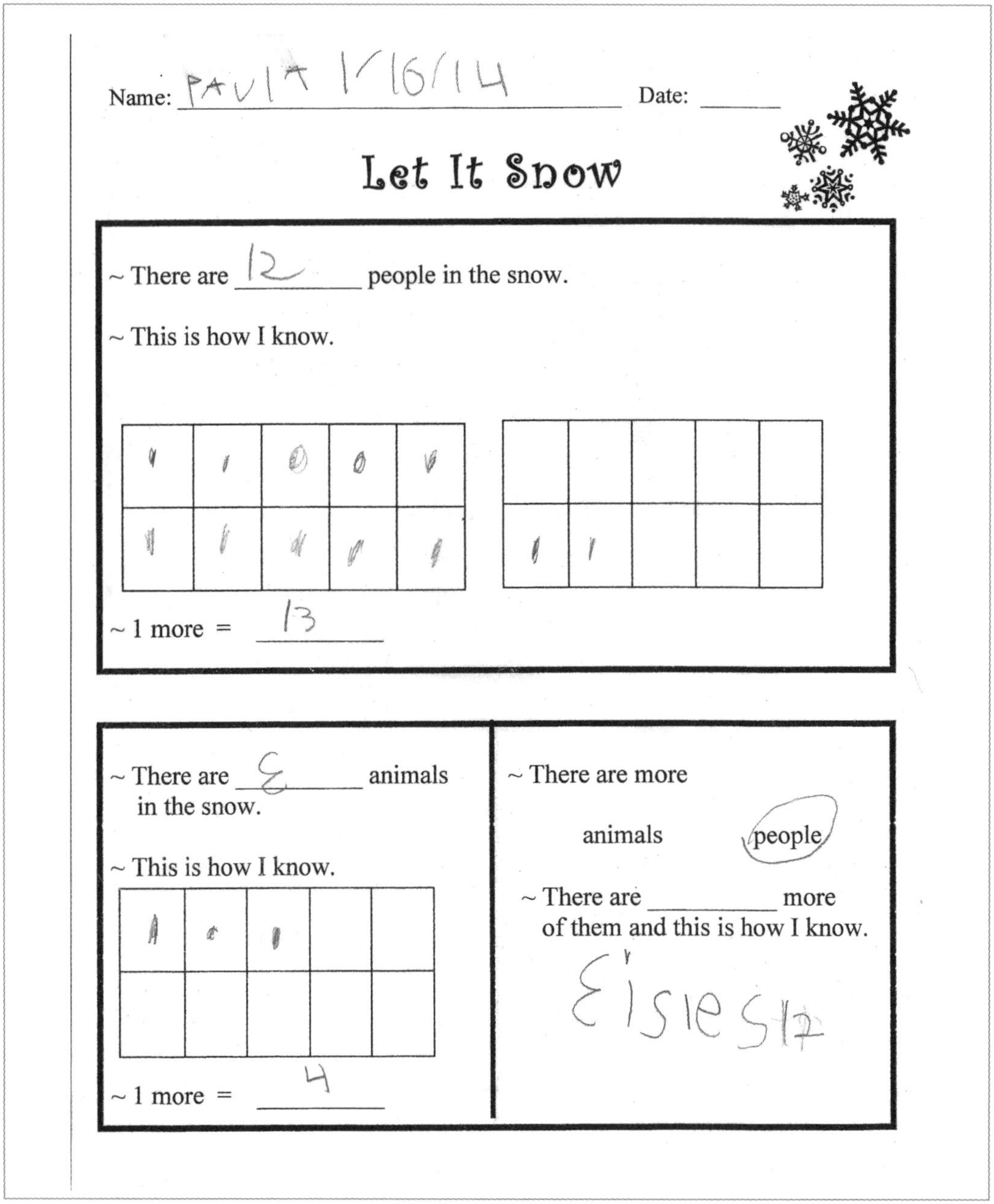

Name: PAULA 1/16/14 _____ Date: _____

Let It Snow

~ There are ___12___ people in the snow.

~ This is how I know.

1	1	0	0	1
1	1	1	1	1

1	1			

~ 1 more = ___13___

~ There are ___8___ animals in the snow.

~ This is how I know.

1	1	1		

~ 1 more = ___4___

~ There are more

animals (people)

~ There are _____ more of them and this is how I know.

Eisies 17

FIGURE 5.6
Jonathan's work on the "Let It Snow" problem

Name: _JOnathan_____ Date: _1/16/14_ ❄❄

Let It Snow

~ There are ___12___ people in the snow.

~ This is how I know.

~ 1 more = ___13_____

~ There are ___3___ animals
  in the snow.

~ This is how I know.

~ 1 more = ___4_____

~ There are more

   animals   (people)

~ There are ___15___ more
   of them and this is how I know.

Used the 2 numbers
and added them

FIGURE 5.7

Eyram's first page of work on the "Let It Snow" problem

Name: __Eyram__   Date: _1-16-14_

Let It Snow

~ There are ___12___ people in the snow.

~ This is how I know.

~ 1 more = ___13___

~ There are ___3___ animals in the snow.

~ This is how I know.

~ 1 more = ___4___

~ There are more

animals   (people)

~ There are ___9___ more of them and this is how I know.

Eyram's next step was to use ten frames to "just show 24 by 2 ten frames and 4 more on another one and put 6 more from the 12 animal feet to finish up that ten frame and then 6 more on another ten frame and that makes 36 in all."

CLASSROOM TEACHER REFLECTIONS — KRISSY LANIER, KINDERGARTEN

▶ Lesson Reflection

At the beginning of the school year, most of my students were having their first experience with school. Collectively there was little concept of number, number patterns, or patterns in general. It made sense for me and for them to use "tools" to show "how many," as this gave visual models to help with difficult concepts. My students learned within days the power of a five frame and quickly moved into using ten frames to extend their concept of number. I saw some of their developing confidence in using tools within this lesson. All of them were successful in using ten frames to show the number of people and animals. Many were able to use ten frames or counters or even the number line to find one more. I really loved the way that Eyram solved and described how he found the total number of footprints. The overall progress of my students in using tools to solve problems that might once have been beyond them is undeniable.

▶ MP5 Reflection

As I think back over this year from my perspective in June, I see that giving my students exposure to solving problems—interesting problems—with a variety of tools such as dice, dominoes, fingers, ten frames, and other manipulatives has given them a solid foundation in number. After working a problem with any number of tools, they are now questioning and testing the responses they make, checking for errors, and using mental math to see if answers are reasonable. They say things like, "I see a ten frame in my head and you said to take away two, so I see two missing on the ten frame, which means it is eight." There is so much meaning attached to their thinking and ideas. Another benefit is that they are now okay with making mistakes and show a desire to work through problems using different tools. They are pushing themselves out of their comfort zones, and it is great to see them doing that!

COMMENTS ABOUT MP5 FROM OTHER CLASSROOM TEACHERS

Grade Two Teacher: I believe that students need to be taught explicitly that many of the "things" we use to help us in math are tools of the trade. Paper and pencil, dominoes, rulers, counters, and base ten blocks are just a few of the tools we can use. Once my students became comfortable with the terminology this year, I had to help them realize that sometimes it is more efficient to use one tool over another. For example, can we solve forty-six minus twenty-three using counters? Yes, we can, but does that open us up to making mistakes by counting incorrectly because we have too many counters? Yes, it does. A more efficient strategy might be subtracting in parts—partial differences—or using tools that can better represent larger numbers like base ten blocks. At first, this was difficult for students to grasp. Many students find a tool they like and then hold on to that tool for dear life. They may not trust a more efficient tool to help them with their reasoning. Reinforcing MP2 can help students cross this bridge and be more confident with the tools they select.

Grade Three Teacher: This seems like the easiest of the MPs to understand. I have always believed that it is important for students at every grade level to use tools in math. For me the challenge is finding the time to introduce new tools to my students that move them past using the "standard" ones of base ten blocks, pattern blocks, and things like square-inch tiles. I am trying to get my students to see estimation as a tool, as well as things like diagrams, tables, and graphs. I am also trying to get them to see and believe that a tool is only as good as its user and that they need to use it for a purpose and not just because it is fun to use.

COMMENTS ABOUT MP5 FROM STUDENTS

Stella, Kindergarten Student: We can use our fingers as tools to find answers. They're great because we can always find them!

Andrew, Grade Two Student: You can use one tool to do a problem and then use a different one to check your answer. I like to use the number line to check my answers to adding and subtracting with blocks.

Sonia, Grade Three Student: Tools are everywhere. We can see and use them at school, at home, or at a friend's house. Base ten blocks are great, math games can be tools, and I sometimes go online to find out things in math.

MATHEMATICAL PRACTICE 6:
ATTEND TO
PRECISION

"I meant what I said and I said what I meant. . . . An elephant's faithful, one hundred per cent!"

—HORTON THE ELEPHANT IN HORTON HATCHES THE EGG

OVERVIEW

It's not always easy to say what we mean and to mean all that we say. Even though this is another Mathematical Practice with only a few words, the meaning is far-reaching and has many layers. When I first read the words of this MP, I immediately thought that attending to precision in mathematics was mostly about getting the "right" answers—those that are accurate, exact, correct. After I thought about it a bit, however, I began to realize that MP6 is about much more than that. Yes, of course, an element of it *is* about getting the right answers, but it is important that we all move beyond that component and help our students move beyond it as well. We must help them see that an essential part of thinking mathematically lies in how we communicate and share that thinking, and that this is where precision is key.

If you remember this Dr. Seuss story about Horton, you remember that Horton is adamant about sticking to what he said, because it has meaning for him, and therefore, he believed it had meaning for others. How often do we see and hear our students challenged in communicating their thinking to others as they search for the right words to explain what they have done to solve a problem and struggle even more to find the words to justify why they have done what they've done? Are they really saying what they mean and meaning what they say? What do they mean when they say, "I timesed it"? Does that give an accurate mathematical description of what they have done? Do they know what they mean by that, and do others know what they mean? How about when someone gives an answer such as, "It's about 37" or "It's about 248.956"? Is either of those an "about" answer? In most cases they are not, yet it is important to note that the level of precision needed depends on the particular situation.

This is where it is critical for students to see that they are moving along a continuum of being able to communicate mathematically in such a way that they can clarify their own thinking and allow others to understand their thought processes. They are accruing the skills to do so, and attention to MP6 will serve them well.

GOALS

The three major goals of this Mathematical Practice focus on students being able to

1. use mathematically specific language (terms, definitions, properties) both orally and in writing to express mathematical thinking and reasoning explicitly, with a level of clarity that allows it to be followed by others;

2. recognize and use mathematical symbols, units of measure, and labels in diagrams and explanations of thinking; and

3. perform calculations with accuracy and efficiency while determining the level of precision called for in a problem (estimate, exact, exact to the nearest whole, ten, and so on).

▶ Goal 1

To use mathematically specific language (terms, definitions, properties) both orally and in writing to express mathematical thinking and reasoning explicitly, with a level of clarity that allows it to be followed by others (Figure 6.1)

▶ Importance of This Goal

Language allows us to communicate, to share, and to connect with one another. We do that via common vocabulary made up of words and terms that have meaning we have de facto agreed upon, thus allowing us to "commune" with each other. Although this is true for all parts of life, it has particular implications for classroom life. As a matter of fact, research does more than suggest a simple link between language and learning, summed up quite nicely by Laura Varlas,

FIGURE 6.1
Goal 1

MATHEMATICAL PRACTICE 6:
ATTEND TO PRECISION

Goal 1: Use mathematically specific language (terms, definitions, properties) both orally and in writing to express mathematical thinking and reasoning explicitly, with a level of clarity that allows it to be followed by others

G—Goal	**O—Observe**	**L—Listen**	**D—Do**
GOAL: *I CAN* STATEMENTS	OBSERVE STUDENTS DOING:	LISTEN FOR STUDENTS SAYING:	DECIDE WHAT TO DO

• I can use math words to share my thinking.
 	
• I can use precise mathematical terms to share my thinking clearly so others will understand.
	• Using specific math terms orally and in written form
	
	• Listening to other students and noting their language
	
	• Listening to and checking themselves for precision of language
	
	• Creating a clear chain of reasoning to convey mathematical ideas to themselves and others
		• We can use our fingers to count on, and that will make us be exact.
		
		• She said "more than" and I said "greater than," but they mean the same thing.
		
		• I timesed 23 by 2—I mean, I multiplied 23 by 2.
		
		• I drew a bar model for ½ and another one for ⅜. Then I compared the two and saw that ½ is equal to ⅘, and when I added that to ⅜, the sum was easy to find: ⅝.
			• Ask
			
			  What is the mathematical term for that?
			
			  Can you be more precise?
			
			  What math terms did you hear in _____'s explanation?
			
			  What's the difference between . . . [example number sentence and equation]?
			
			  What terms are easy for you to use and understand? Hard to use and understand?
			
			• Model a precision of language—ensure that you are using the most specific terms.
			
			• Be aware of language pitfalls that contribute to misunderstandings for all students (borrow, reduce, etc.).
			
			• Scaffold mathematical language development for students for whom English is a second language.
			
			• Provide ample opportunities for students to "talk math" by engaging in conversations, student to student, student to class, student to teacher, etc.
			
			• Support the creation and use of a student-constructed "math word wall."

who says, "Academic vocabulary is one of the strongest indicators of how well students will learn subject area content" (2012, 1).

In mathematics, we must be careful to model clear and precise language and to expect that of our students as well. Students use too many words and phrases (as do we) that can and do promote misconceptions and can be barriers to deep conceptual understanding. Although it may seem efficient in the moment to say *borrow*, for example, and to let students say that, it can be misleading—if someone borrows ten dollars from you, you have an expectation that it will be returned—never mind what it obscures mathematically. I love the way Cathy Seeley thinks about this: "By being careful with our own language and communication, we can also avoid 'temporary mathematics' that may need to be later undone" (2014, 314). I, too, feel strongly about this and provide a few words and terms that I have identified as "outlaws" and that, as such, should not be used (see the NCSM fall 2013 newsletter for a few of them).

▶ Goal 2

To recognize and use mathematical symbols, units of measure, and labels in diagrams and explanations of thinking (Figure 6.2)

▶ Importance of This Goal

This goal is something that teachers have long held in high regard and pay great attention to in their teaching. Some of this attention grows from what happened to us as students. How many of us lost a few points here and there because we didn't label an answer on a test? Although doing well on tests, of course, is important to most students, it is not the main reason it is essential to label our work. It goes back once again to the idea of sharing our thinking with others. When we are explicit and clear in our labeling of answers, diagrams, and so on, we are more likely able to provide a chain of our thinking and reasoning that others can follow.

The same thinking applies to the use of symbols. Students must be aware of the appropriate and strategic use of mathematical symbols and all that they communicate. A common example of an imprecise use of symbols is when a student working on adding 72 and 12 decomposes 12 into 10 and 2 and writes

$$72 + 12 = 72 + 10 = 82 + 2 = 84$$

FIGURE 6.2
Goal 2

MATHEMATICAL PRACTICE 6:
ATTEND TO PRECISION

Goal 2: Recognize and use mathematical symbols, units of measure,
and labels in diagrams and explanations of thinking

G—Goal	**O—Observe**	**L—Listen**	**D—Do**
GOAL: *I CAN* STATEMENTS	OBSERVE STUDENTS DOING:	LISTEN FOR STUDENTS SAYING:	DECIDE WHAT TO DO
• I can use math symbols and labels and know what they mean. • I can use math symbols, units of measure, and labels to share my thinking clearly.	• Writing and reading number sentences with appropriate signs, symbols on whiteboards, on paper, etc. • Writing and reading labels with understanding • Writing, reading, and using mathematical symbols within the context of solving problems • Writing, reading, and using labels in explaining mathematical thinking	• If I have 12, and I add 4 more and get 16 in all, I can show that by $12 + 4 = 16$. • But the answer isn't just 16—it has to have a label, so the answer really is 16 balloons. • $14 < 21$ means that 14 is less than 21 because the arrow is pointing to the left and the smaller number is to the left of a larger one on the number line. • When we multiply 34 and 56, we could decompose this into multiplying tens by tens, tens by ones, and ones by ones. It could look like $(30 \times 50) + (30 \times 6) + (4 \times 50) + (4 \times 6)$. • This measurement is labeled cm^3, so it means we are dealing with volume, because . . .	• Ask *Which mathematical symbols are important in this problem? Which are not?* *Which symbols do you use most often?* *Why did you label the diagram as you did?* *Could you have labeled this differently without changing the solution?* *Which conversions do you know well? Which do you need to learn?* • Model consistent use of symbols, units of measure, and diagrams, and . . . • . . . insist that students do the same. • Give examples and have students give examples of how lack of precision with symbols, labels, etc., can lead to ambiguous and even incorrect solutions. • Add appropriate symbols and units of measure (and grade-level-appropriate conversions) to the class math word wall. • Provide ample opportunities for students to highlight their use of symbols, units of measure, labels, etc.

Written this way, it reads that $72 + 12$ is equal to $72 + 10$ and then that equals $82 + 2$. The final answer is correct, but the notation is not.

Let me throw in a caveat here: although I believe that it is absolutely essential for students to acquire precise vocabulary, to understand the specific meanings of words, to assign labels as they work, and to use symbols precisely and accurately, I maintain that it has to be done along a continuum. This kind of precision develops over time, and we need to give students every opportunity to see and hear it modeled while they build and improve their skills. They need the encouragement to communicate even though they might not be completely precise and accurate. Although this support comes from us as teachers, I also see peers as enormous sources of support and agree with Elham Kazemi and Allison Hintz, who maintain, "It can be quite powerful for a classroom community when students share ideas that aren't quite right yet and seek the help of their classmates" (2014, 12).

▶ Goal 3

To perform calculations with accuracy and efficiency while determining the level of precision called for in a problem (estimate, exact, exact to the nearest whole, ten, and so on) (Figure 6.3)

▶ Importance of This Goal

Accurate calculations are good and hold a place of importance in our mathematics classrooms. I am often surprised, however, and even dismayed when I hear from parents and the public at large that they believe we educators have let go of the "basics." They maintain that this "new" approach to math is more about making children feel good and not so much about knowing how to add, subtract, multiply, and divide correctly—and that we believe that as long as students' answers are close, it's okay.

Obviously, this is not the case. We *do* want students to be able to compute accurately, and further, we want students to do so both efficiently and proficiently. Susan Jo Russell wrote a wonderful article about this soon after NCTM published its *Principles and Standards for School Mathematics* in 2000 that identifies computational fluency as a goal for all students, with fluency comprising three elements: efficiency, flexibility, and accuracy (Russell 2000).

FIGURE 6.3
Goal 3

MATHEMATICAL PRACTICE 6:
ATTEND TO PRECISION

Goal 3: Perform calculations with accuracy and efficiency while determining the level of precision called for in a problem (estimate, exact, exact to the nearest whole, ten, and so on)

G—Goal	**O—Observe**	**L—Listen**	**D—Do**
GOAL: *I CAN* STATEMENTS	OBSERVE STUDENTS DOING:	LISTEN FOR STUDENTS SAYING:	DECIDE WHAT TO DO
• I can make an estimate and give an exact answer. • I can decide if an exact or estimated answer is needed and then calculate correctly.	• Completing mental and written computations with whole numbers with accuracy and relative efficiency (with fingers, objects, representations, etc.—see Content Standards for specifics) • Making reasonable estimates based on prior knowledge • Determining if an estimate is needed or an exact answer is needed • Completing mental and written computations with fractions and decimals with accuracy and relative efficiency— see Content Standards for specifics (4–5)	• I know that 7 take away 2 means I start with all 5 fingers up on one hand and 2 on another; I then put down 2, and that leaves 5. I can show that on my whiteboard, and I can write it with numbers and signs. • I know you don't want the exact answer because you said "about how many," and I know it has to be about 100, because there were 50 cubes yesterday, and this looks like double. • We're looking for how many groups of 5 there are in 46, and because we can skip-count by 5s and get to 45 after 9 counts, then . . . • Adding ⅔ and ¾ we already know the answer is greater than one whole since both fractions are more than ½, so . . .	• Ask *Why is it necessary to be more precise with a calculation sometimes?* *When do you use estimates in your everyday life?* *When do you need exact answers?* *What helped you make this estimate?* *What is a different way you can compute this answer?* • Model how to make decisions about whether to compute mentally, with paper and pencil, or with a calculator. • Model how to determine if an estimated answer is needed or an exact one is needed and, if the latter, to what level of precision (whole number, fractional/decimal remainder, etc.). • Provide opportunities for students to engage in these decision-making situations and have them share and justify how they made decisions. • Discuss and explicitly teach how to make estimates for various contexts and for multiple types of measures (linear, weight, volume, etc.). • Help students move toward more efficient ways to compute by providing scaffolding experiences (for example, moving from adding with counters, to using base ten blocks, to using pictorial representations, etc.).

This is where MP6 comes into play in a big way. Do we want students to be precise in their calculations? A resounding "Yes!" is the answer—and we want much more. We want students to go beyond calculating by rote to questioning the level of precision that is needed for each problem. If you want to know how many buses are needed for a field trip for 150 people and each bus holds 60 people, is an estimated answer of 3 buses sufficient or do you need to have an exact answer of 2½ or 2.5 or 2.50? When measuring for a window blind, is a whole number okay or do you need to know to the nearest tenth or even hundredth? This is when this component of MP6 has real meaning.

CLASSROOM LESSON: GET TO WORK

▶ My Restaurant

Suppose someone asked you to plan a restaurant. Where would you begin, and what would you include? Take a minute and jot down some ideas about what you would need to know to start carrying out such a task. More than likely your list would include the size of the physical space, how much room would be needed for the kitchen, the size of the dining room, how many tables could fit, the size and shape of those tables, and how many people the restaurant could hold. You would have to consider all of those things and more before you could start to think about the menu, the food preparation, prices, and so on—a daunting task for many and certainly a multidimensional one for all.

▶ Classroom Lesson Overview—Take a Look

- Grade: 5

- Focus Content Standard(s): 5.NF.6 Solve real-world problems involving multiplication of fractions and mixed numbers; 5.MD.1 Convert among different-sized standard measurement units within a given measurement system and use these conversions in solving multistep, real-world problems.

- Student Language: Solve real-world problems involving multiplying with fractions and whole numbers and converting measurement units.

- Focus Math Practice: MP6: Attend to Precision

- I Can Statement: I can use math symbols, units of measure, and labels to communicate my reasoning clearly.

- Lesson Setup:

When Miss Murphy first introduced the restaurant problem to her students, they immediately showed a great deal of enthusiasm. She began by asking them what they thought would be needed to plan a new restaurant. The initial answers centered on food: whether it would be ethnic or "just American," and what kinds of desserts and main courses would be on the menu. Some students even wondered about how to make the food safe for customers with allergies. Miss Murphy then asked how they could plan the actual layout of the restaurant and what that would entail. Students began discussing how much room they had and how the space could be arranged, as well as what kinds of tables they would use: square, rectangular, round, and so on.

Miss Murphy drew attention to the Focus Content Standards in Student Language, the Focus Math Practice, and the I Can statement, all written on the board, and asked students to read each one aloud. She then asked the students if they could see the connection between the written goals and the task they were facing. They did, and seemed eager to start.

Before she placed the students into groups of two, three, or four, Miss Murphy presented guidelines and requirements that included a recording sheet to be completed by the group members, with the understanding that they would construct a model on graph paper that needed to be approved by her before they could make a large-scale drawing on poster paper. Students were told they would also be creating and designing a menu for their restaurants. Additionally, they were told that this would be a two- to three-day project, with a class "restaurant showcase" as a culmination.

▶ Classroom Lesson Observations—Look Some More

Talk about focused and on-task students! The "buzzing" was at times quiet and thoughtful, while at other times it was punctured by bursts of excitement and a proliferation of students saying, "Ooh-ooh, I've got a great idea!" They settled into the "design" phase fairly quickly, and it was evident that trial and error was a necessary first step for many of them in terms of the mathematical requirements. When they realized that at least one-third of the space had to be reserved for the kitchen, some wanted to construct it so that the total space was a multiple of three "because that just makes it much easier." There was a range in total area from 990 square feet to 1,419 square feet, with many partners agreeing on 1,386 as a "nice number to work with."

As the students worked on the task, it became clear to them that they needed to be "really, really precise," according to Juliet and Kira, who went on to say, after much editing, reworking, and checking back in on the requirements, "This was really challenging at first. Our rough draft helped, but we still had to make a lot of renovations before we could open." (See Figure 6.4 for Juliet and Kira's work.) It was also clear to all of the students that there were many tools available to help them complete this task. They were using rulers, yardsticks, meter sticks, calculators, and even sticky notes as temporary labels to flesh out their rough drafts. Nathan and Izzy talked about drawing the boxes "roughly at first but then we had to be really accurate when we did the real measuring, so we used rulers and also counted the squares on the graph paper."

Although all of the students were aware of their units of measure, only some of them attached labels and units of measure to every work product. (See Figure 6.5 for Trinidy and Denise's work.) It was also interesting to note how different students focused on the level of precision needed for a specific question. When they had to convert feet to yards, for example, students did it differently. Trinidy and Denise converted 249 feet into 82 yards with "r 2," a remainder of 2, whereas Kira and Juliet converted 292 feet into 97 1/3 yards. (See Figure 6.6 for Kira and Juliet's work.)

CLASSROOM TEACHER REFLECTIONS — SHANNON MURPHY, GRADE FIVE

▶ Lesson Reflection

This lesson was done near the end of the school year, and I'm glad it was. I think that by then, many of my students had a better idea of the need for "attending to precision" and why it is important. As I watched them start this

FIGURE 6.4

Kira and Juliet's work on the "My Restaurant" problem

Student Name: Kira & Juliet

My Restaurant – Part 1

DESIGN – Using grid paper, design a restaurant that includes a commercial kitchen and a dining area. At least 1/3 of your space should be the kitchen. Fill your dining space with tables and chairs. You will need a combination of dining tables styles – 2 tops, 4 tops, 6 tops. Tables should be square or rectangular in format. *Write a digit in each table stating how many people can eat at that table*. Each chair should be shown as a circle inside one square on your grid paper. Leave space around the perimeter of your restaurant.

a. How many people can dine in your restaurant? 100 people

b. If your restaurant is ½ full, how many people can dine? 50 people

c. During a busy night your restaurant fills up 2 ½ times. How many people could be served? 250 people

d. What is the area of your entire restaurant? 1,312 sq.ft

e. What is the area of your dining space? 864 sq.ft

f. What is the area of your kitchen space? 448 sq.ft

g. If each square on grid = 2 feet, what is the perimeter of your dining space? 292 sq.ft.

How many yards? 97 ⅓ yd How many inches? 3,504 in

h. If each square on grid = 2 feet, what is the perimeter of your kitchen? next

How many yards? next How many inches? next

Use colored pencils to complete your design and attach your work to this sheet. Be sure to do your best work!

FIGURE 6.5

Trinidy and Denise's work on the "My Restaurant" problem

Student Name: Trinidy&Denec

My Restaurant – Part 1

DESIGN – Using grid paper, design a restaurant that includes a commercial kitchen and a dining area. At least 1/3 of your space should be the kitchen. Fill your dining space with tables and chairs. You will need a combination of dining tables styles – 2 tops, 4 tops, 6 tops. Tables should be square or rectangular in format. *Write a digit in each table stating how many people can eat at that table*. Each chair should be shown as a circle inside one square on your grid paper. Leave space around the perimeter of your restaurant.

a. How many people can dine in your restaurant? 80 people

b. If your restaurant is ½ full, how many people can dine? 40 people

c. During a busy night your restaurant fills up 2 ½ times. How many people could be served? 200 people

d. What is the area of your entire restaurant? 1386 sq ft

e. What is the area of your dining space? 992 sq. ft

f. What is the area of your kitchen space? 394 sq. ft

g. If each square on grid = 2 feet, what is the perimeter of your dining space? 248 ft

How many yards? 82 yd² How many inches? 2976 in

h. If each square on grid = 2 feet, what is the perimeter of your kitchen? 176 ft

How many yards? 58 yd² How many inches? 174 in

Use colored pencils to complete your design and attach your work to this sheet. Be sure to do your best work!

FIGURE 6.6

Kira and Juliet's restaurant design

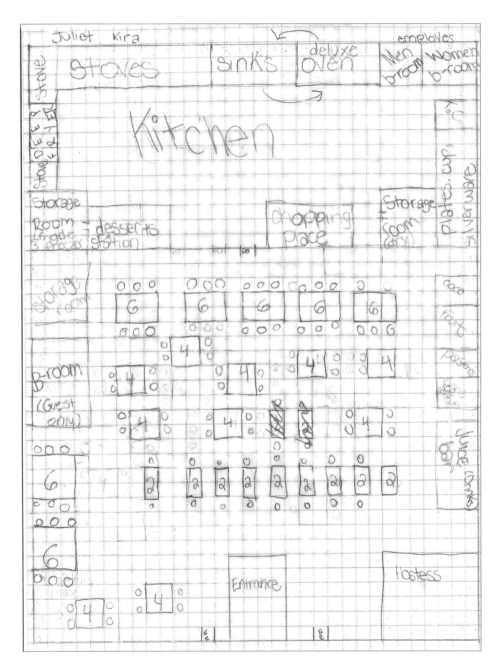

project and heard them talk to each other as they planned various parts of it, I was seeing and hearing things that I probably wouldn't have seen and heard at the beginning of the year. They seemed to understand better that sometimes you have to be very precise and very accurate. Although many of them wanted to rush through parts of it, enough of them pulled their partners back and made them check for accuracy in measurements, check to make sure they were meeting all the requirements I had put in for them, and check for correct conversions and calculations. I don't think they could have been as thorough at the beginning of the year.

▶ MP6 Reflection

I think that even though it might sound easy at first, Attend to Precision is a hard concept to grasp if it is not explicitly taught. When I had conversations with my students about this at the beginning of the year, I found that they mostly saw this through the example of measurements. They knew that it didn't make sense to guess or estimate how big boards need to be when building a house— that to build a house successfully, you had to measure with precision. It was with language that I had some issues. I think that I (and probably many others) assume that our students understand the words we use as teachers of math, but I have found that this is not always true. I am now more aware of the importance of checking for understanding.

COMMENTS ABOUT MP6 FROM OTHER CLASSROOM TEACHERS

Kindergarten Teacher: As this year has progressed, I have been intertwining all eight practices in my teaching at different levels and to different degrees. MP6 is one that rolled out surprisingly well in my class. Language is generally challenging to kindergartners, and academic vocabulary is hard. But now here in April, my students are asking their peers and even me to be more precise in daily discussions: "Mrs. Lanier, I don't understand the question. Could you be more precise?" They have come to realize that there is meaning attached to every word, and their goal is to have others understand them. Learning to be "precise" has given them an inner voice that pushes them to think before they explain, leading them to have deeper conceptual understanding as well as improved communication.

Grade Four Teacher: I don't think I am alone in thinking that this MP looks pretty straightforward at first but has much more to it when you dig down deeper. I am becoming more aware of the need to ensure that my students use correct, specific, appropriate math vocabulary. I am becoming more aware that this has to be done both orally and in written form. I am becoming aware that this needs to be done when they ask questions, when they describe a strategy, and when they defend their answers. I am becoming aware that I need to continue to focus on this practice both as a teacher and a learner.

COMMENTS ABOUT MP6 FROM STUDENTS

Daisy, Kindergarten Student: It's good to use your fingers. It's good to use counters, because it's good to be precise, because that means it's good to be exact!

Noble, Grade One Student: It's important to *attend to precision*, because if you rush, you will get all your work wrong, and then you will need to do it again!

Colin, Grade Two Student: Checking my work lets me be precise and lets me find mistakes and maybe not do those mistakes. I pay attention to my words, and it keeps me from doing and telling the problem the wrong way.

CHAPTER (7)

MATHEMATICAL PRACTICE 7:
LOOK FOR AND MAKE USE OF STRUCTURE

A mathematician, like a painter or poet, is a maker of patterns. If his patterns are more permanent than theirs, it is because they are made with ideas.

—*G. H. HARDY, ENGLISH MATHEMATICIAN*

OVERVIEW

This quote comes from someone who loved mathematics to its core. Hardy was passionate about number theory and mathematical analysis—pure mathematics—and celebrated the aesthetics of math. I like to think that Hardy would have had a special affinity for MP7. To discern a pattern, one must look closely at the underlying structure, and then step back to gain perspective, generate some ideas about the nature of the structure—the regularities that can be seen as well as envisioned beneath and within—apply those ideas, and then assess to determine if the pattern holds.

What is wonderful about this MP is that it offers a way to look at the world both within and well beyond the classroom walls. Anyone who has worked with prekindergartners and kindergartners knows that once students learn the word *pattern*, almost everything is a pattern to them! Even though that may not always be the case, there are patterns hiding within patterns, alongside of patterns, underneath patterns, shooting off from patterns. The joy of their discovery can allow students to flow between drilling down to the core of a pattern and uncovering its structure, and widening out to a more global and generalized view.

GOALS

The three major goals of this Mathematical Practice focus on students being able to

1. identify and describe numeric and geometric patterns and use their structure to make predictions and hypotheses;

2. use perspective to consider the whole of something as well as to identify components of the whole; and

3. apply prior knowledge and structural understanding to new problem situations.

▶ Goal 1

To identify and describe numeric and geometric patterns and use their structure to make predictions and hypotheses (Figure 7.1)

▶ Importance of This Goal

The structure of the pattern helps in making predictions about what might come next and/or what might happen further out; in this way we move from the specific to the general. To do this, students must examine relationships between and among the components of a problem, whether those relationships are in terms of numbers or shapes. They must exercise both flexibility and tenacity to unlock patterns. Something to remember here is that although it is important for students to have multiple opportunities to name, replicate, and extend patterns as a basis for laying the groundwork for algebraic reasoning, the full benefit of this will be actualized "only if we prompt children to attend to the mathematical properties and describe the repeating structures in mathematically predictable ways" (McGarvey 2013, 571).

▶ Goal 2

To use perspective to consider the whole of something as well as to identify components of the whole (Figure 7.2)

▶ Importance of This Goal

Often, students appear to demonstrate that they "understand" a concept by completing a set of problems and getting the correct answers. Although a student may appear as if he has a solid understanding of place value and

FIGURE 7.1
Goal 1

MATHEMATICAL PRACTICE 7:
LOOK FOR AND MAKE USE OF STRUCTURE

Goal 1: Identify and describe numeric and geometric patterns and use their structure to make predictions and hypotheses

G—Goal	O—Observe	L—Listen	D—Do
GOAL: *I CAN* STATEMENTS	OBSERVE STUDENTS DOING:	LISTEN FOR STUDENTS SAYING:	DECIDE WHAT TO DO
• I can use number and shape patterns to help me understand math ideas. • I can use patterns in numbers and shapes to find relationships and to make predictions.	• Using ten frames, hundreds charts, etc., to count to 5 and 10, to count by fives and tens, etc. • Noticing and using repetitions in numbers and shapes • Identifying and explaining numerical patterns related to addition and multiplication (on addition/multiplication tables, hundreds charts, in student-constructed tables) • Finding the area of figures that grow in a pattern by identifying and using the relationships of the measures involved	• One ten frame is 10, 2 ten frames are 20, and I know that means 4 ten frames are 40 and 8 ten frames are 80! • Look what happens when I count by nines on the hundreds chart—down a row and over one to the left each time. • I saw that when I add 5 to an even number, I get an odd number, but when I add 5 to an odd number, it's always even. • This is a pattern, and I can see that the area is increasing by the same amount each time because . . .	• Ask *What did you notice first?* *Why do you think that works? Will this always work?* *How do you know that . . . ?* *Which mathematical ideas (concepts, properties, etc.) can/did you use?* *How can you organize the information?* • Discuss what makes a pattern a pattern (allows predictions to be made, shortcuts to be used, etc.). • Do "out loud" thinking to model how you work to see and find relationships and patterns (showing that some information is irrelevant, making predictions and then testing them, etc.). • Provide problems that are similar to ones students have solved before so they can take advantage of previously learned knowledge by applying it to new problems and situations. • Provide easy access to age-appropriate tools (counters, inch tiles, charts, calculators, etc.) • Stress the importance of students communicating their findings.

FIGURE 7.2
Goal 2

MATHEMATICAL PRACTICE 7:
LOOK FOR AND MAKE USE OF STRUCTURE

Goal 2: Use perspective to consider the whole of something as well as to identify components of the whole

G—Goal	**O—Observe**	**L—Listen**	**D—Do**
GOAL: *I CAN* STATEMENTS	OBSERVE STUDENTS DOING:	LISTEN FOR STUDENTS SAYING:	DECIDE WHAT TO DO
• I can build bigger numbers and shapes from smaller numbers and shapes, and take them apart. • I can compose and decompose numbers and shapes in multiple ways.	• Using a number line to see that 10 is made up of 10 ones, 2 fives, 5 twos, etc. • Exploring and explaining the patterns in doubles and halves and how those can be used to explain other relationships • Composing and decomposing numbers and shapes in multiple ways • Using pattern blocks to find relationships between and among shapes	• I can get to 10 in more than one way: it can be 10 hops when I move one at a time, or I can do two hops of 5 each. • When you double a number, you can either add it twice or multiply by two. Double 2 is 4, and 2 times 2 is 4. Then double 4 is 8, and that's the same as when you add 2 four times. • Finding half of something is just making two equal parts. Half of 20 is 10, and half of that is 5. If I add 5 four times, it gets me back to 20. • There are 3 triangles in a trapezoid, which makes a triangle equal to $\frac{1}{3}$ of a trapezoid. A trapezoid is half of a hexagon, which makes a triangle $\frac{1}{6}$ of a hexagon.	• Ask *What did you look at first?* *Did you see it the same way as your partner?* *How can you explain what you saw?* *Why is it important to look at something in more than one way?* *Can you describe what you see in a different way? Can you show it with words? With pictures? With numbers?* • Model what it takes to "step back" and see the whole as well as to see the parts of things; if appropriate, define and use the term *perspective*. • Allow time for students to share with the class the patterns they see as well as how they came to see them. • Acknowledge that it takes practice to see things in different ways. • Validate working both from whole to part and from part to whole.

correctly say that 234 equals 2 hundreds plus 3 tens plus 4 ones, that same student may experience difficulty seeing that 234 can also be thought of as 23 tens and 4 ones. It is a challenge for him to shift his thinking from viewing individual components of a whole so that he sees it through another lens. Karl Duncker, a Gestalt psychologist, coined the term *functional fixedness,* which essentially means a narrowed view of an object that does not allow one to see or use that object in any way other than the originally intended or most common one (Duncker 1945). I am sure that many of you see this in students who can think of only one way to look at a number, to perform an operation, to describe a shape, or to solve a problem. They are stuck in that one way and often construct a mental barrier that prohibits them from considering a different perspective. When students circumvent this functional fixedness, as I apply it to math, it is easier for them to move more fluidly from both whole-to-part and part-to-whole thinking and to regard an alternative view as viable, thereby increasing the likelihood that they will use patterns and structure to inform and expand their mathematical thinking.

▶ Goal 3

To apply prior knowledge and structural understanding to new problem situations (Figure 7.3)

▶ Importance of This Goal

One of my greatest joys is when I see a student use something she already knows to solve something she seemingly does not know. I am sure you celebrate when a student realizes how applying her already learned skill of using doubles and halves can couple with her ability to decompose numbers when she has to multiply. What a thrill when this student verbalizes that 4 times 23 is the same as doubling 2 times 23, which is 46, and that 46 plus 46 is just double 45 plus 2 more! When students become aware of how efficient it is to use what is already in their backpacks of knowledge, so to speak, they experience greater success in solving more complex problems. They come to realize that they do not always have to start, like Maria in *The Sound of Music* "at the very beginning, a very good place to start." They activate their thinking from files they hold already, sort through them, make an association, and build on that connection to construct a new pathway to new knowledge. This prior knowledge, or

FIGURE 7.3
Goal 3

MATHEMATICAL PRACTICE 7:
LOOK FOR AND MAKE USE OF STRUCTURE

Goal 3: Apply prior knowledge and structural understanding to new problem situations

G—Goal	O—Observe	L—Listen	D—Do
GOAL: *I CAN* STATEMENTS	OBSERVE STUDENTS DOING:	LISTEN FOR STUDENTS SAYING:	DECIDE WHAT TO DO
• I can use easier problems to solve harder problems. • I can use what I know to find out what I don't yet know.	• Adding/subtracting 1 to or from a collection of objects and identifying the count as the next or previous counting number • Using knowledge of place value and number relationships to perform calculations mentally or in written form • Noticing similarities and differences and then using them to discover and explore • Using patterns within one operation to identify and explore patterns in another operation	• I know that 8 plus 1 more is the next number—9—so 14 plus 1 more is 15. • 96 plus 56 is 90 + 50, which is 140, and then add 12 for the 6 + 6 to get 152 for the total. • Adding an odd and an even number always results in an odd number, but multiplying an odd number by an even number always results in an even number. • 8 × 10 is 80 and 8 × 100 is 800, so 8,000 ÷ 100 is the same as . . .	• Ask *Are you seeing any similarities to something you have noticed before?* *How can something you already know help you with something harder?* *How does this relate to . . . ?* *What is a rule that might describe what you notice?* *Now that you've described this orally, can you show what you notice visually? With numbers?* • Model how to use something you are already familiar with to help in finding out something you don't yet know. • Introduce a class mantra of sorts: "Use what you know to find out what you don't yet know!" • Highlight when students use prior knowledge in solving a new problem. • Present problems that are rich in mathematical structure and encourage students to explore.

background knowledge, is not only the "glue that makes learning stick," according to ReLeah Lent, but also "an essential component in learning because it helps us make sense of new ideas and experiences" (Lent 2012, 30).

CLASSROOM LESSON: GET TO WORK

▶ Square Thinking

You may want to solve this problem yourself before reading the next section. Take the time to complete the problem to the degree that you would want your students to do so. As you work, make note of which of the Mathematical Practices you are employing. Pay particular attention to MP7 and identify when, where, and how you specifically did (or did not) look for and make use of structure.

> One square table can seat 4 students; two square tables can seat 6 when the tables are pushed together. Given this arrangement:
> **A**nalyze to find how many students can sit at 3, 10, 50, and 100 tables.
> **B**rainstorm how you can solve the problem.
> **C**ommunicate how you solved this and what you discovered.

▶ Classroom Lesson Overview—Take a Look

- Grade: 4

- Focus Content Standard: 4.OA.5 Generate a number or shape pattern that follows a given rule. Identify apparent features of the pattern that were not explicit in the rule itself.

- Student Language: Identify and use a number pattern to solve a problem.

- Focus Math Practice: MP7: Look For and Make Use of Structure

- I Can Statement: I can use patterns in numbers to find relationships and to make predictions.

- Lesson Setup:

After students read the content standards and other information on the board, Ms. Hanson asked, "What does 'using structure' mean to you?" A discussion followed of what it might mean as well as a more specific discussion about what it means to look for relationships between and among numbers. One student thought that it had to do with buildings. Another thought it had to do with making a table or chart to use in solving a problem. Additional exchanges centered on how the use of known relationships at a simple level can be helpful in solving more complex problems.

Ms. Hanson then asked the students to name some of the tools they have used in the past to solve problems. They generated a list that included assorted counters, base ten blocks, pattern blocks, number lines, hundreds charts, calculators, tables, and drawings. She followed this with, "How do you choose which tool is the right one, the appropriate one?" One of the students shared that he often changes his mind about which tools to use as he gets further into a problem. When Ms. Hanson asked if anyone else had done that, many hands went up, and the group discussed the benefits of changing one's mind.

Ms. Hanson told students they would be solving a problem that she had had to think about for a while before she had solved it—which intrigued them. She presented the problem to them and stressed the importance of using words, numbers, and/or pictures to give evidence for and to prove their answers, and to justify their thinking.

Ms. Hanson placed the students into pairs, and they set off to solve it. All students were given the basic problem, and some were given a more challenging problem to solve after they had completed the initial problem.

▶ Classroom Lesson Observations—Look Some More

As students started to work in pairs, it was interesting to watch which ones immediately used square-inch tiles to model the problem. Once a few pairs did this, however, most of the others did the same. It was interesting to note the similarities and differences in how the student pairs solved the problem and how well they looked for and then used the structural patterns to help them do so.

Several pairs laid out the tiles and recorded each result as they went along, adding one "table/tile" each time with varying results. Take a look at Valerie's work (Figure 7.4). When asked to describe what she noticed, she and her partner noted, "It is going up by two each time because more tables mean two more kids can sit." After a while, the pair decided that they could just fill in the chart by counting by twos to determine the number of people who could be seated. See if you can find where they made their mistake. Although this pair saw a pattern and used it to some degree, it did not result in complete accuracy in terms of all parts of the problem. They recognized and used the pattern, but a counting error resulted in some inaccuracies in some parts.

In contrast, several groups just found the answers for 3 and 10 first, recorded their work in different ways, and then were able to make use of the pattern they identified to solve the rest of the problem. Regine (Figure 7.5) and her partner showed the work for 3 and 10 with drawings and tick marks. From there, they noticed that it was a combination of multiplication and addition that yielded their results. They were able to step back a bit and see the whole of the problem. Regine then floated a hypothesis revolving around the pattern they saw and "kept on trying and it was correct," allowing the two of them to use what they found for 3 and 10 to determine the answers for 50 and 100.

Alina and her partner (Figure 7.6) saw the structure in the problem almost immediately. They confirmed their thinking about what they saw with 3 tables by making another drawing depicting 10 tables. From there, they were able to identify a rule and make a generalization, which they articulated with clarity. When asked what would happen if they had pentagonal tables, the two used what they had discovered about square tables and applied it to the conditions of the new problem (Figure 7.7) with a slight modification (instead of multiplying by 2 as they had for a square table, they multiplied by 3). They were so excited by their discoveries, they kept on going.

FIGURE 7.4

Valerie's work on the "Square Thinking" problem

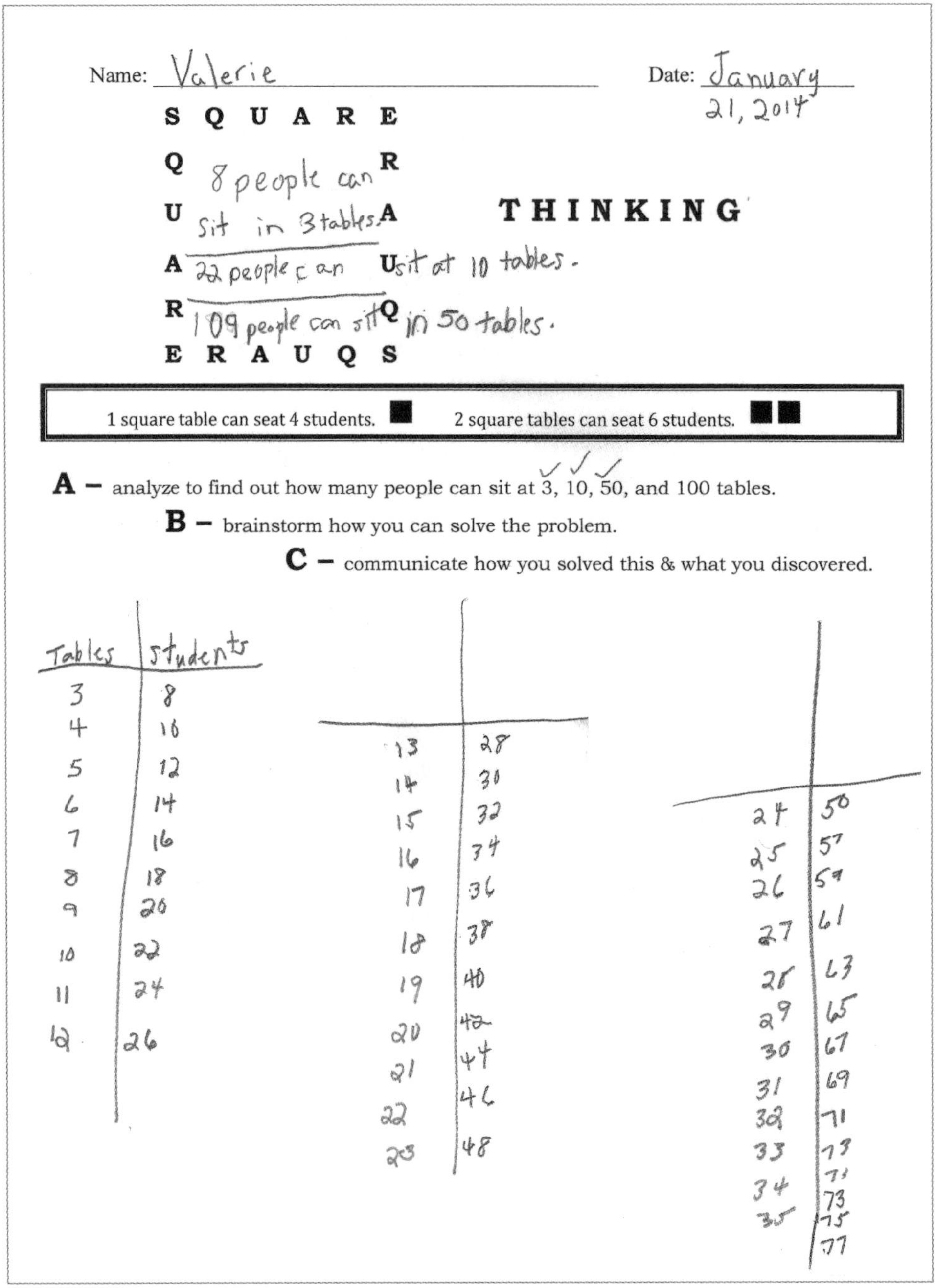

Name: _Valerie_____   Date: _January 21, 2014_

S Q U A R E

Q   R
   8 people can
U sit in 3 tables.A   **T H I N K I N G**

A 22 people can   U sit at 10 tables.

R   Q
   109 people can sit in 50 tables.
E   R   A   U   Q   S

| 1 square table can seat 4 students. ■ | 2 square tables can seat 6 students. ■ ■ |

A – analyze to find out how many people can sit at 3, 10, 50, and 100 tables.

   B – brainstorm how you can solve the problem.

      C – communicate how you solved this & what you discovered.

Tables	Students
3	8
4	10
5	12
6	14
7	16
8	18
9	20
10	22
11	24
12	26

13	28
14	30
15	32
16	34
17	36
18	38
19	40
20	42
21	44
22	46
23	48

24	50
25	57
26	59
27	61
28	63
29	65
30	67
31	69
32	71
33	73
34	71
35	73
	75
	77

FIGURE 7.5

Regine's work on the "Square Thinking" problem

Name: Regine   Date: 1-21-2014

```
S   Q   U   A   R   E
Q                   R
U                   A          THINKING
A                   U
R                   Q
    E   R   A   U   Q   S
```

| 1 square table can seat 4 students. ■ | 2 square tables can seat 6 students. ■■ |

A – analyze to find out how many people can sit at 3, 10, 50, and 100 tables.

B – brainstorm how you can solve the problem.

C – communicate how you solved this & what you discovered.

$\times 2 + 2$

A - 3 = ▢▢▢ = 8

$50 = 50 \times 2 + 100 + 2 = 102$

$100 = 100 \times 2 = 200 + 2 = 202$

10 = ▢▢▢▢▢▢▢▢▢▢ = 22

50 = 102

100 = 202

B - 1-4, 2-6, 3-8

1×2 2×2 3×2
$2 + 2$ $4 + 2$ $6 + 2$

C - I figured out that the problem was multiply 2 add 2. Frist, I noticed that $1 \times 2 = 2$ $2 + 2 = 4$. When, I figured out I kept on trying it and it was correct soon I figured that it was a multi-step problem.

FIGURE 7.6

Alina's work on the "Square Thinking" problem

Name: Alina   Date: 1/21/13

S Q U A R E

Q   R

U   A   T H I N K I N G

A   U

R   Q

E R A U Q S

1 square table can seat 4 students. ■   2 square tables can seat 6 students. ■ ■

A – analyze to find out how many people can sit at 3, 10, 50, and 100 tables.

 B – brainstorm how you can solve the problem.

  C – communicate how you solved this & what you discovered.

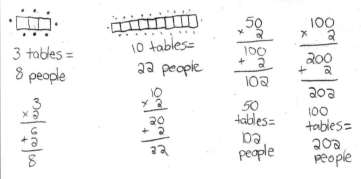

3 tables =
8 people

$$\begin{array}{r} 3 \\ \times\ 2 \\ \hline 6 \\ +\ 2 \\ \hline 8 \end{array}$$

10 tables=
22 people

$$\begin{array}{r} 10 \\ \times\ 2 \\ \hline 20 \\ +\ 2 \\ \hline 22 \end{array}$$

$$\begin{array}{r} 50 \\ \times\ 2 \\ \hline 100 \\ +\ 2 \\ \hline 102 \end{array}$$

50 tables=
102 people

$$\begin{array}{r} 100 \\ \times\ 2 \\ \hline 200 \\ +\ 2 \\ \hline 202 \end{array}$$

100 tables=
202 people

It's a multi-step pattern.
First you have to multiply the
number of tables ×2. Next
you have to add 2 to your
product.

FIGURE 7.7

Alina's work on the new problem

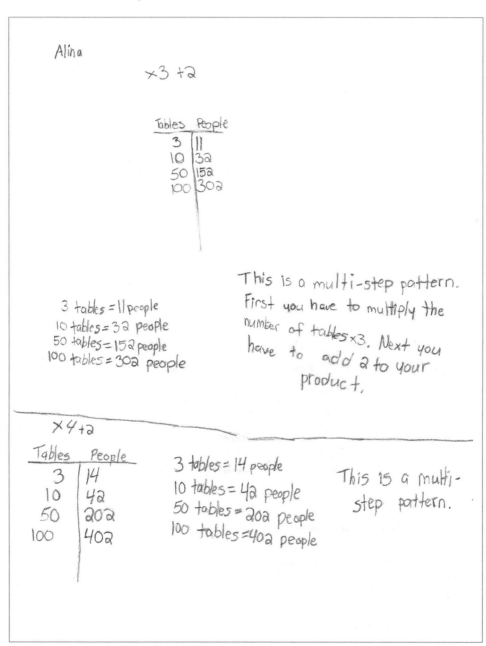

Alina

×3 +2

Tables	People
3	11
10	32
50	152
100	302

3 tables = 11 people
10 tables = 32 people
50 tables = 152 people
100 tables = 302 people

This is a multi-step pattern.
First you have to multiply the
number of tables ×3. Next you
have to add 2 to your
product.

×4 +2

Tables	People
3	14
10	42
50	202
100	402

3 tables = 14 people
10 tables = 42 people
50 tables = 202 people
100 tables = 402 people

This is a multi-
step pattern.

CLASSROOM TEACHER REFLECTIONS — BROOKE HANSON, GRADE FOUR

▶ Lesson Reflection

As the kids worked on the problem, it was interesting for me to see how each of the partner groups got started. Some knew right away that using the inch tiles would help them see the problem more easily, and some had absolutely no idea how to start. Also, some knew that making some sort of a chart or table as they worked could help them see a pattern within the problem. It seemed as if this helped to unlock the problem for many of them and let them see what was actually happening in terms of the numbers, and from there, many could then name a pattern or rule. That part was great! I realized, however, that several of my students were struggling and were looking to other students to model what they had done.

It was also great to see what some of the partner groups did when I extended the problem and asked them to find out what would happen if the tables used were a different shape. I was blown away by the way some of them attacked this challenge and solved it!

▶ MP7 Reflection

This has been an interesting Mathematical Practice for me to begin to wrap my brain around. I made some obvious inferences about what it means to *look for and make use of structure*, but I really could not articulate it much beyond saying that it has something to do with looking for and naming patterns and then using the patterns to solve problems. Thinking of it in terms of the three major goals has helped, but I know that I need to continue to fine-tune my thinking about it. In addition, I have come to realize that if I am challenged by grasping the nuances of this MP, then I have to work extra hard at making sure I can model it in ways that make it clear to my students.

COMMENTS ABOUT MP7 FROM OTHER CLASSROOM TEACHERS

Grade One Teacher: This Mathematical Practice makes a lot of sense to me, especially here in the younger grades. I see that making use of the structure in our number system is a great way to help students understand the relationships and then how to capitalize on using them. Once they see they know the answer to 3 plus 4, they also know the answer to 4 plus 3, 7 minus 4, and 7 minus 3! And it's even greater when they make use of the fact that learning 4 plus 4 can easily come by knowing both 3 plus 3 and 4 plus 4. When structure is used, more of mathematics is more accessible to more people.

Grade Four Teacher: This MP came alive for me this year in particular as I realized how important it was for me to have base ten blocks readily available in tenths and hundredths so that my students could really make use of the structure. This was an eye-opener, and I am beginning to see more clearly the importance of pushing my students—all of them, not just the ones I think are more ready for it—to actively look for patterns and structure and then do something with what they find.

COMMENTS ABOUT MP7 FROM STUDENTS

Danny, Grade One Student: I use my doubles to help me with doubles plus 1, and then I can also use them to find doubles minus 1, and that makes it really easy.

Emmanuel, Grade Three Student: I do this when I use an easy problem to help me understand a harder problem—it makes the problem useful.

Denise, Grade Five Student: Just like a bridge has beams to support it as a structure, looking for a pattern and then using that structure is a good support to help you solve harder problems.

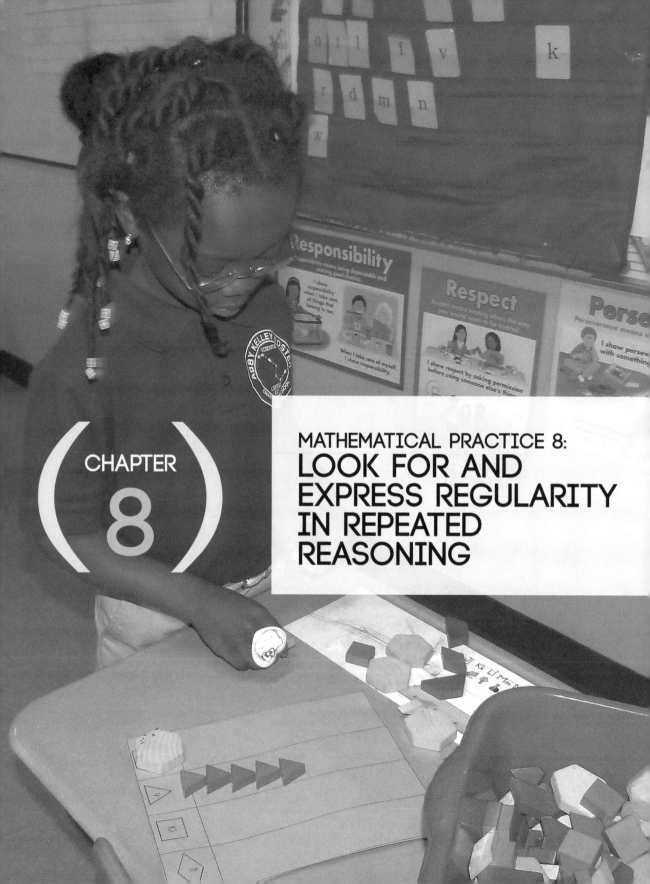

MATHEMATICAL PRACTICE 8:
LOOK FOR AND
EXPRESS REGULARITY
IN REPEATED
REASONING

The essence of mathematics is not to make simple things complicated, but to make complicated things simple.

—STANLEY GUDDER, MATHEMATICS PROFESSOR

OVERVIEW

This Mathematical Practice challenges most people, and to be honest, it took me a great deal of time to move beyond my first "understanding" of it. Initially, I was comfortable chalking it up to noticing when something is repeated in terms of work with numbers, such as when adding two numbers and one is 9 (take one away from the other addend to make the 9 a 10). I was happy enough with using the regularity of that procedure to my advantage. I also saw that I could connect this MP, for example, to the repetition that happens when dividing a multiple of 10 by 3 and then using that repetition to make my work simpler and more efficient.

I now see MP8 more fully than I first did. There is no denying that it still is about looking *for* and looking *at* the patterns that permeate our number operations, especially those regularities in computational algorithms that can be used to make subsequent work with numbers easier and more efficient. MP8 reaches out further than that, however, and extends to work with unit rates and ratios, and to the examination of patterns and regularities in geometry, such as when dealing with the slope and the sum of angles in polygons, for example.

Mathematical Practice 8 casts an even wider net when it is seen as a vehicle for allowing us to make generalizations based upon the information gathered from "smaller," more specific discoveries of regularities. This is where MP8 kicks into high gear and gets to the "essence of mathematics." Harder and more complicated mathematics becomes simpler and more accessible through the application of the knowledge that comes by way of identifying and using regularities in repeated reasoning.

GOALS

The three major goals of this Mathematical Practice focus on students being able to

1. recognize repetitions in calculations as meaningful and useful in finding "shortcuts";

2. apply a broader use of patterns/regularities and use their structure to make generalizations to solve analogous problems; and

3. attend to where they are in a problem and check to ensure their actions and results make sense as they move toward a solution.

▶ Goal 1

To recognize repetitions in calculations as meaningful and useful in finding "shortcuts" (Figure 8.1)

▶ Importance of This Goal

Picture this: you have been spending some time in class having students explore an algorithm that is more conceptually based than the procedurally based one most of us were taught—let's say partial differences, for example. The next day a student comes into class all excited to show you "a trick my dad taught me—it's a shortcut," convinced that you probably don't know about it. Sound familiar? Let me be clear: I am thrilled that parents and children are spending time together around math, and I am thrilled that children are aware that there *are* shortcuts in computational procedures. I am less than thrilled, however, that most of these shortcuts are devoid of conceptual understanding and that when asked to explain how and why the shortcuts work, students respond with blank stares and shrugged shoulders.

In the past, the majority of elementary school mathematics revolved around computation. There is general consensus today, however, that the reality of what our students need in terms of mathematical understanding and thinking moves far beyond being good in arithmetic. This does not mean that instructional time on computation is eliminated but that it is reduced. This can be accomplished with the result of students becoming proficient by having them notice and take

FIGURE 8.1
Goal 1

MATHEMATICAL PRACTICE 8:
LOOK FOR AND EXPRESS REGULARITY IN REPEATED REASONING

Goal 1: Recognize repetitions in calculations as meaningful and useful in finding "shortcuts"

G—Goal	**O—Observe**	**L—Listen**	**D—Do**
GOAL: *I CAN* STATEMENTS	OBSERVE STUDENTS DOING:	LISTEN FOR STUDENTS SAYING:	DECIDE WHAT TO DO
• I can see when things repeat and I can make a rule. • I can notice repetitions, make a rule that fits, and then use that rule as a shortcut.	• Making observations about the behaviors of numbers • Making observations about the behaviors of operations • Finding and articulating regularities, especially in computational algorithms • Using repetitions to make sense of the mathematics and to find shortcuts based on mathematical reasoning	• Counting by 2 means to say a number, skip the next number, and then say the one after that. It doesn't matter if you start with an even or odd number—it's still the same. • When I add one-digit numbers, I just add ones; when I add two-digit numbers, I add tens and ones; so for three-digit numbers, I have to add hundreds, tens, and ones. • Multiplying two two-digit numbers is like doing four multiplication problems—ones by ones, ones by tens, tens by ones, and tens by tens. • One whole pizza divided in half gives 2 slices, 2 pizzas in halves gives 4, and 3 pizzas gives 6, so 10 must give 20, and . . .	• Ask *Is there anything here that repeats?* *How did you solve this problem?* *Is there a more efficient way to solve this?* *How does this relate to . . . ?* *What happens if you try this with smaller numbers? With larger ones?* • Say explicitly that the math that students are learning makes sense, follows patterns, and is filled with regularities—things that happen over and over—which can be used to make even more sense of the mathematics. • Model how taking note of patterns and regularities can lead to finding shortcuts in work with numbers and operations. • Resist showing shortcuts to students. • Encourage parents to resist showing shortcuts to their children. • Provide opportunities for students to share their "Aha!" shortcuts and encourage them to learn from their classmates' discoveries.

advantage of the regularities so that they, in Seeley's words, "generalize the procedures they're learning so that they don't have to learn the same procedures over and over again." Seeley goes on to say, "In other words, we want to teach students a procedure that works for all kinds of numbers, not just for three-digit numbers this year, four-digit numbers the next year, and so on" (2014, 337).

▶ Goal 2

To apply a broader use of patterns/regularities and use their structure to make generalizations to solve analogous problems (Figure 8.2)

▶ Importance of This Goal

The key to this component is that although playing with and exploring patterns is important, it is when students identify a regularity, name and articulate it, and then step back and see how it can be applied to something more complex by generalizing it that the power is felt. I agree with Lynn McGarvey, who says, "One of the noted obstacles along the route to algebraic thinking is the tendency to apply recursive reasoning to patterning" (2013, 566). She maintains that although students can build and extend a pattern and are successful in predicting what comes next, it is often difficult for them to go further. McGarvey pulls from research by Thomas Carpenter and John Lannin (Carpenter et al. 2005; Lannin 2005) to note that students "struggle to find a general rule or relationship so they can determine the element or value at any position in a pattern" (McGarvey 2013, 566). This is where we have to push our students beyond just predicting what comes next, so that they can engage in mathematical reasoning.

When young students are asked to show different ways to represent the twenty-fourth day of school, for example, and they write $23 + 1 = 24$, $22 + 2 = 24$, $21 + 3 = 24$, and so on, they are noticing a regularity. It is when they can articulate, however, that this works because one addend becomes smaller by one and the other becomes larger by one that they are applying the "reasoning" part of this MP. That reasoning is extended even further when they express that this will also work if one addend decreases by two while the other increases by two and they go on to note other regularities that can be applied. What I love most about this component is the joy of discovery that students display when they "unlock" such underlying mathematical principles and ideas.

FIGURE 8.2
Goal 2

MATHEMATICAL PRACTICE 8:
LOOK FOR AND EXPRESS REGULARITY IN REPEATED REASONING

Goal 2: Apply a broader use of patterns/regularities and use their structure
to make generalizations to solve analogous problems

G—Goal	O—Observe	L—Listen	D—Do
GOAL: *I CAN* STATEMENTS	OBSERVE STUDENTS DOING:	LISTEN FOR STUDENTS SAYING:	DECIDE WHAT TO DO
• I can use a pattern in an easy problem to solve a harder problem. • I can see a pattern or regularity, make a rule, and then use it to solve more difficult problems.	• Using something they notice and already know to find something they do not yet know with certainty • Exploring, building, and extending patterns • Moving beyond exploring patterns, etc., with an eye toward identifying the regularities and finding the mathematics underlying them • Sharing their reasoning, even their first attempts at identifying patterns and regularities	• Five plus 5 is 10, 6 plus 4 is 10, and 7 plus 3 is 10. Start with a double and then add one more to the first number and take one away from the second number, and you still get the same answer. Let's see if this works for all doubles . . . • To find 162 – 58, I can first find the difference between 58 and 62, which is 4, and then just add 100 to that, so the answer is 104, because . . . • Multiplying a one-digit number by 10 means that the digit moves from the ones place to the tens place. Multiplying a two-digit number by 10, the digit in the tens place moves to the hundreds place and the digit in the ones place moves to the tens place. The two-digit number becomes a three-digit number with a 0 in the ones place. This goes on when . . . • In this table, the first term has 7, the second has 13, the third has 19 . . . The numbers increase by 6, but it would take too long to figure out what the twentieth term would be, so there must be a rule we can use to figure it out.	• Ask *What are you noticing here that looks the same as . . . ?* *Can you step back and see the mathematics that is here?* *What math do you already know that can help with this?* *What do you think might happen if/when you . . . ?* *How can you extend this?* • Provide examples of using prior knowledge to relate to something new. • Present problems for which you have not yet "taught" specific strategies, and give students time to work collaboratively to move toward solutions. • Give ample "airtime" and have students share what they notice, what hypotheses they make, etc. • Set the expectation that students must make connections to the mathematics involved in the regularities and patterns they discern. • Stress that although there may be more emphasis on seeing repeated reasoning in work with numbers and operations at the elementary level, this type of reasoning extends to work with fractions, ratios, measurements, geometry, etc.

▶ Goal 3

To attend to where they are in a problem and check to ensure their actions and results make sense as they move toward a solution (Figure 8.3)

▶ Importance of This Goal

This component of MP8 is interwoven with MP1: Make Sense of Problems and Persevere in Solving Them, as well as with MP3: Construct Viable Arguments and Critique the Reasoning of Others. Deep learning and understanding of mathematical concepts take place within contexts and are embedded in problem situations. The days when elementary school mathematics was primarily arithmetic—what I call naked number computation—are gone. If we want our students to believe that mathematics is essential to their lives, that it is relevant to their lives now and will be in the future, that it is something that has meaning and does make sense, then we must immerse them in problem-solving opportunities that require them to find the meaning and the sense in what they are doing by way of their mathematical reasoning.

Bill McCallum, one of the authors of the Common Core, is central to Illustrative Mathematics (2014), a resource that is vital to helping teachers understand and implement the Common Core. Offered within this resource is *Standards for Mathematical Practice: Commentary and Elaborations for K–5*, a work still in progress, where it is noted for MP8 that "As they work to solve a problem, mathematically proficient students maintain oversight of the process, while attending to details. They continually evaluate the reasonableness of their intermediate results" (Illustrative Mathematics 2014, 10). This is where students are asked to step back and see the big picture as they work and determine whether their reasoning is on target. David Sousa, in *How the Brain Learns Mathematics*, maintains that we need to devote more time to developing true mathematical reasoning in students and that part of it is metacognition, "which is thinking about what you are doing, why you are doing it, and making adjustments as needed." He further says that "Knowledge and performance are not reliable of either reasoning or understanding. For deep understanding, the what, the why, and the how must be well-connected. Then students can attach importance to different patterns and engage in mathematical reasoning" (2008, 123).

FIGURE 8.3
Goal 3

MATHEMATICAL PRACTICE 8:
LOOK FOR AND EXPRESS REGULARITY IN REPEATED REASONING

Goal 3: Attend to where they are in a problem and check to ensure their actions and results make sense as they move toward a solution

G—Goal	O—Observe	L—Listen	D—Do
GOAL: *I CAN* STATEMENTS	OBSERVE STUDENTS DOING:	LISTEN FOR STUDENTS SAYING:	DECIDE WHAT TO DO
• I can keep track of my thinking and see if it makes sense. • I can keep track of where I am in a problem and know where I am headed.	• Stopping along the way as they solve problems and explaining their work with objects, drawings, etc. • Taking the time to make sure their work thus far makes sense • Stopping intermittently as they complete interim steps to explain to themselves and others • Not giving up when they check either an intermediate answer or a final one and determine it is wrong and must start again	• Sixty-nine plus 12 is 72, because 60 plus 10 is 70 and 2 more to make 12 makes it 72—but wait, that can't be right, because 69 is almost 70 to start with, and if you're adding 12, then . . . • I think we have to keep adding, because even though we are getting closer, we have not gotten to where we need to be for this . . . • No way is that right—we are only adding 168 and 74. The answer can't be in the 300s, because both numbers would have to be more than 100 for that to be possible . . . • We multiplied to find the total amount that would have been spent on the backpacks before the sale, and now we have to find what the cost would be based on the sale price. But there are two different types of backpacks, so now we have to . . .	• Ask *How do you know you are heading in the right direction?* *How does your work thus far compare to _____'s work?* *Why do you think your plan makes sense?* *What is the big question in this problem? What are the little questions?* *How did you change or revise your thinking when you realized something did not make sense?* • Underscore the critical component of this MP as sense-making. • Model how to check your steps as a problem is solved, ensuring that intermediate results make sense. • Explicitly model how to see both the "forest and the trees"—how to keep track of the details while not losing sight of the desired end. • Explicitly tie this component of Mathematical Practice 8 to MP1. Ask students for thoughts about this first. • Highlight how this component also relates to MP3.

CLASSROOM LESSON: GET TO WORK

▸ Go Figure

Try this one before you take a look at how the lesson went in Shannon Murphy's fifth-grade classroom. It is a great problem that I have used many times, and yet I am continually surprised by the excitement it generates.

> Choose two numbers whose difference is 2.
>
> Find their product.
>
> Find the number between the two original numbers.
>
> Square it.
>
> Subtract 1 from the square number.
>
> Follow the above procedure several times. Show your work and describe what you notice.
>
> Do you think this always works? Why or why not? Build your argument and defend your thinking.

▸ Classroom Lesson Observations—Take a Look

- Grade: 5

- Focus Content Standard(s): 5.OA.3 Analyze (numerical) patterns and relationships.

- Student Language: Analyze and explore numerical patterns.

- Focus Math Practice: MP8: Look For and Express Regularity in Repeated Reasoning

- I Can Statement: I can identify a pattern or regularity and use reasoning to make a rule to help solve problems.

- Lesson Setup:

The students in Ms. Murphy's class had been asked all year to use mathematical reasoning as they solved problems. This was still a newer concept to them, but they generally accepted that they would be asked to look carefully at problems to see if they could find any "clues" that would help them find a solution. When asked why this was important, one student immediately answered that this would cut down on the amount of work she would have to do for other problems that might follow that could be similar to the one just solved.

Miss Murphy set the problem into motion by having students read the Focus Content Standard in Student Language, the Focus Math Practice, and the I Can statement, all written on the board. Students were then asked a series of questions: *What happens when you add two even numbers? Two odd numbers? One even and one odd? Will those results always be the same? Why or why not? What about when you subtract? Multiply? Divide?* These questions and answers were the foundation of a discussion about how numbers in our number system operate according to various theories and so on, and are governed by rules, principles, and properties.

All the students in the class worked through the example of the problem context with the numbers 3 and 5 together. Students wrote on individual whiteboards as the problem was demonstrated on the large whiteboard. Miss Murphy partnered the students and set them to work, reminding them as they started that they were to look for a commonality, a regularity, as they tried this with several sets of numbers that could be used as a basis for their reasoning.

▶ Classroom Lesson Observations—Look Some More

It was fascinating to watch the students get started on the problem. Some of the partners decided that it made sense for each of them to try it with different sets of numbers and then compare their results; other pairs wanted to work on the same set of numbers simultaneously and then compare results. Whereas many of them worked on their whiteboards, erased after they compared, and then tried again with other sets of numbers, some did all of their work on paper, "so we can see and remember what we did." It was also interesting to see how students dealt with initial uncertainty and even confusion. Jasmine said, "This is hard, but I guess that's normal if you don't know something at first." She and her partner kept at it and were successful in coming to an answer and supporting their reasoning. Jacob was clearly feeling a bit overwhelmed at first but did not let that deter him. "I felt confused for a while, but then I started to understand a little, then a little more, and by the end, I understood a lot more," he said. "The tiles and the calculator really helped my thinking because I could see what was happening better."

Almost all the students found that the procedure always works with the product of the two numbers whose difference is 2 having a difference of 1 from the square of the number between the two original numbers. Most played it relatively safe and tried it with smaller numbers they were comfortable with, whereas others pushed past their comfort zones. After Victoria and her partner had tried it with one- and two-digit numbers, she wanted to try it with a three-digit set and was thrilled with what she found. (See Figure 8.4 for Victoria's work.) Bridget and her partner were very methodical moving from two one-digit numbers, to one one-digit and a two-digit, and then to two two-digit numbers, one set beyond their comfort level. (See Figure 8.5 for Bridget's work.) Nuna and her partner included some trials with negative numbers and maintained it worked. Nuna successfully showed how and why by demonstrating with tiles and showing a 2-by-4 rectangular array with eight tiles and a 3-by-3 square with nine tiles beside it, even showing how if one tile is removed from the square, the 2-by-4 could result (Figure 8.6). Her written description (Figure 8.7) was not as complete as her oral one. Marcus and his partner also tried a variety of numbers, including negative numbers. What is also interesting here is that Marcus pointed out how it will not work when the difference between the two original numbers is 1. (See Figures 8.8 and 8.9 for Marcus's work.) It would be great to push him a bit further on this to see if he could find a regularity here as well.

CLASSROOM TEACHER REFLECTIONS — SHANNON MURPHY, GRADE FIVE

▶ Lesson Reflection

I have to admit that I was not sure what the answer to the problem was at first, so I was unsure what to expect from my students. It was definitely challenging for them, because I don't think they had been asked to come at an understanding

FIGURE 8.4

Victoria's work on the "Go Figure" problem

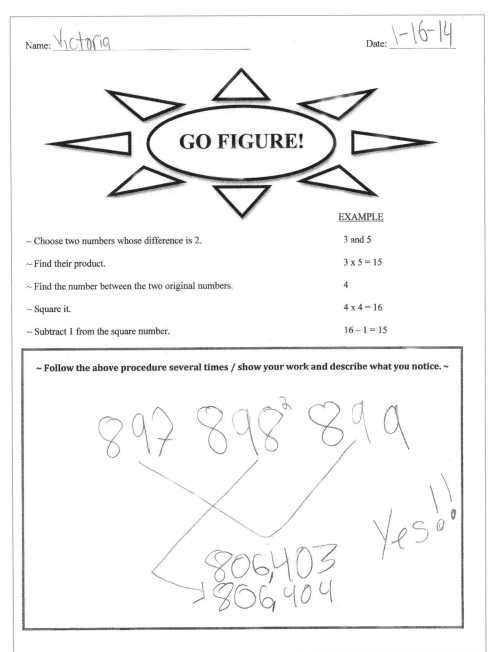

FIGURE 8.5

Bridget's work on the "Go Figure" problem

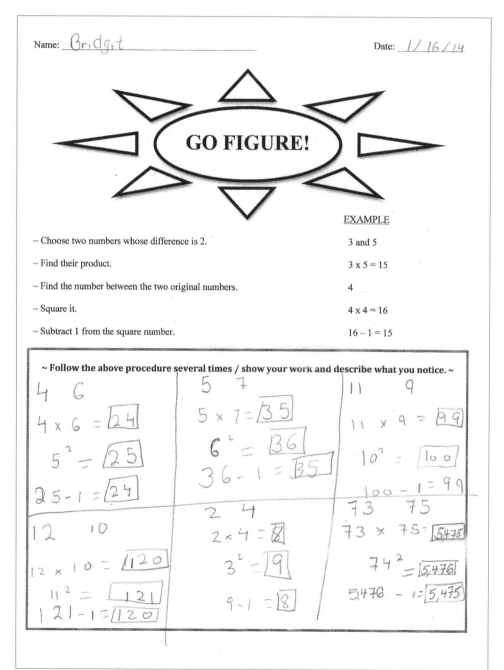

Name: Bridgit   Date: 1/16/14

GO FIGURE!

	EXAMPLE
~ Choose two numbers whose difference is 2.	3 and 5
~ Find their product.	3 x 5 = 15
~ Find the number between the two original numbers.	4
~ Square it.	4 x 4 = 16
~ Subtract 1 from the square number.	16 – 1 = 15

~ Follow the above procedure several times / show your work and describe what you notice. ~

4   6
$4 \times 6 = \boxed{24}$
$5^2 = \boxed{25}$
$25 - 1 = \boxed{24}$

12   10
$12 \times 10 = \boxed{120}$
$11^2 = \boxed{121}$
$121 - 1 = \boxed{120}$

5   7
$5 \times 7 = \boxed{35}$
$6^2 = \boxed{36}$
$36 - 1 = \boxed{35}$

2   4
$2 \times 4 = \boxed{8}$
$3^2 = \boxed{9}$
$9 - 1 = \boxed{8}$

11   9
$11 \times 9 = \boxed{99}$
$10^2 = \boxed{100}$
$100 - 1 = \boxed{99}$

73   75
$73 \times 75 = \boxed{5,475}$
$74^2 = \boxed{5,476}$
$5,476 - 1 = \boxed{5,475}$

FIGURE 8.6

Nuna's work on the "Go Figure" problem

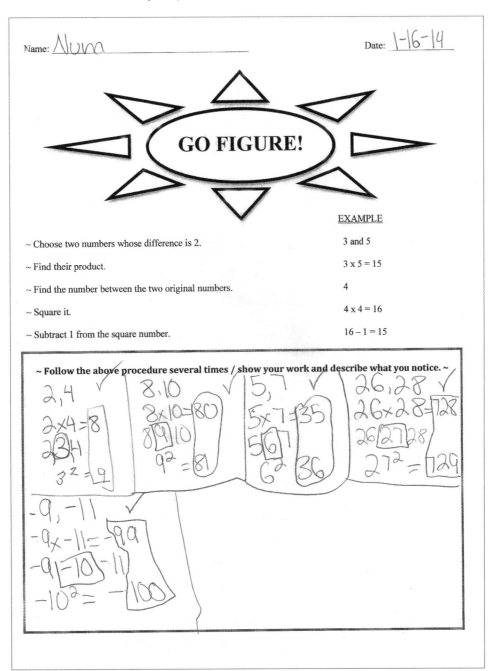

Name: Nuna   Date: 1-16-14

GO FIGURE!

	EXAMPLE
~ Choose two numbers whose difference is 2.	3 and 5
~ Find their product.	3 x 5 = 15
~ Find the number between the two original numbers.	4
~ Square it.	4 x 4 = 16
~ Subtract 1 from the square number.	16 − 1 = 15

~ Follow the above procedure several times / show your work and describe what you notice. ~

2,4 ✓
2×4=8
234
$3^2 = 9$

8,10 ✓
8×10=80
8910
$9^2 = 81$

5,7 ✓
5×7=35
567
6^2 36

26,28 ✓
26×28=728
26 27 28
$27^2 = 729$

-9,-11 ✓
-9×-11= 99
-9 -10 -11
$-10^2 = -100$

FIGURE 8.7
Nuna's written description

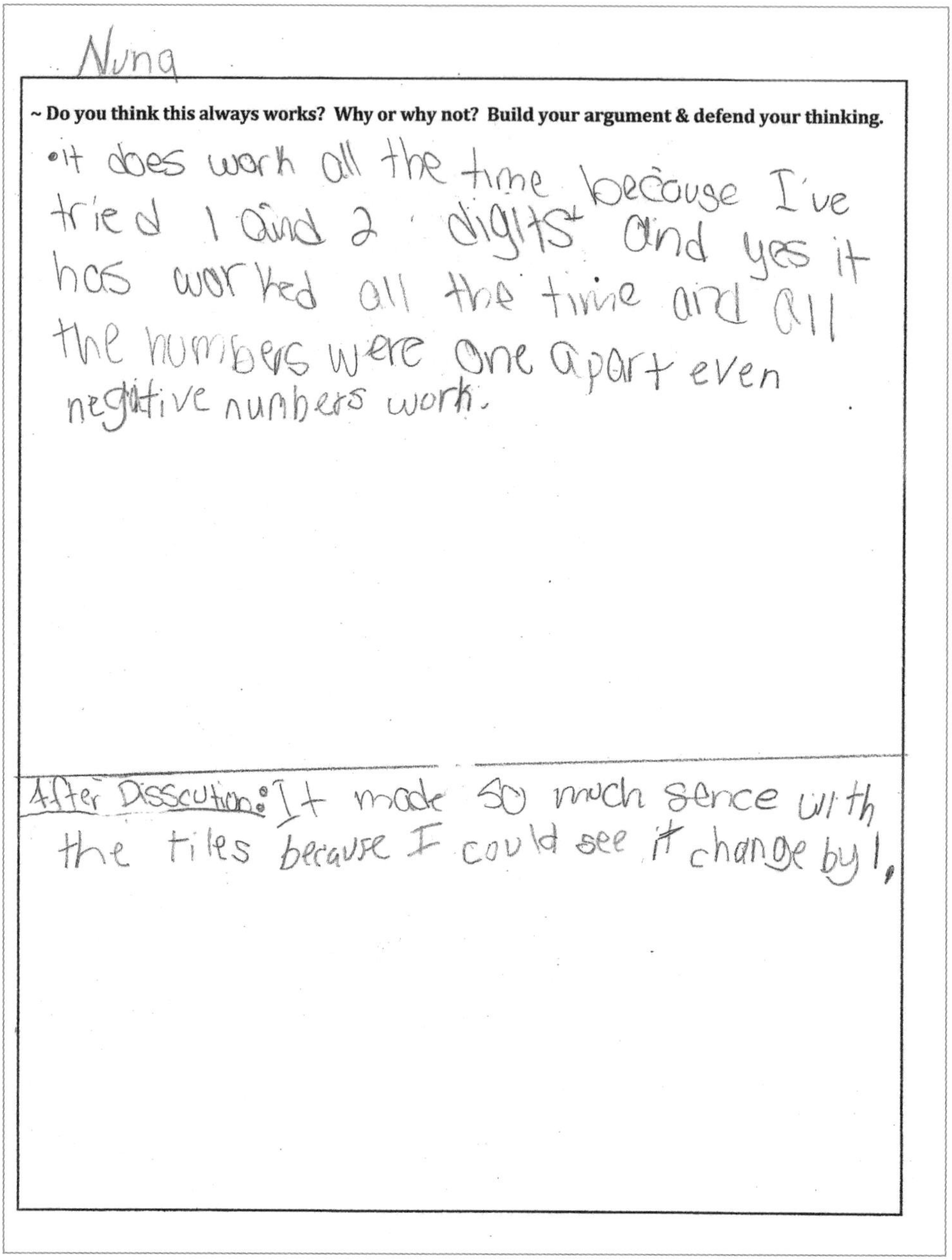

Nuna

~ Do you think this always works? Why or why not? Build your argument & defend your thinking.

• it does work all the time because I've tried 1 and 2 digits and yes it has worked all the time and all the numbers were one apart even negative numbers work.

After Disscution: It made so much sence with the tiles because I could see it change by 1,

FIGURE 8.8

Marcus's work on the "Go Figure" problem

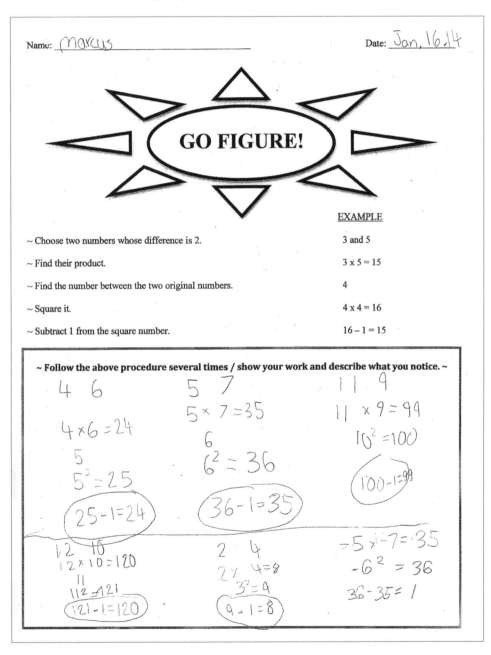

Name: Marcus   Date: Jan. 16. 14

GO FIGURE!

	EXAMPLE
~ Choose two numbers whose difference is 2.	3 and 5
~ Find their product.	3 x 5 = 15
~ Find the number between the two original numbers.	4
~ Square it.	4 x 4 = 16
~ Subtract 1 from the square number.	16 – 1 = 15

~ **Follow the above procedure several times / show your work and describe what you notice.** ~

4 6

$4 \times 6 = 24$

5

$5^2 = 25$

$25 - 1 = 24$

5 7

$5 \times 7 = 35$

6

$6^2 = 36$

$36 - 1 = 35$

11 9

$11 \times 9 = 99$

$10^2 = 100$

$100 - 1 = 99$

12 10

$12 \times 10 = 120$

11

$11^2 = 121$

$121 - 1 = 120$

2 4

$2 \times 4 = 8$

$3^2 = 9$

$9 - 1 = 8$

$-5 \times -7 = 35$

$-6^2 = 36$

$36 - 35 = 1$

FIGURE 8.9

Marcus's written description

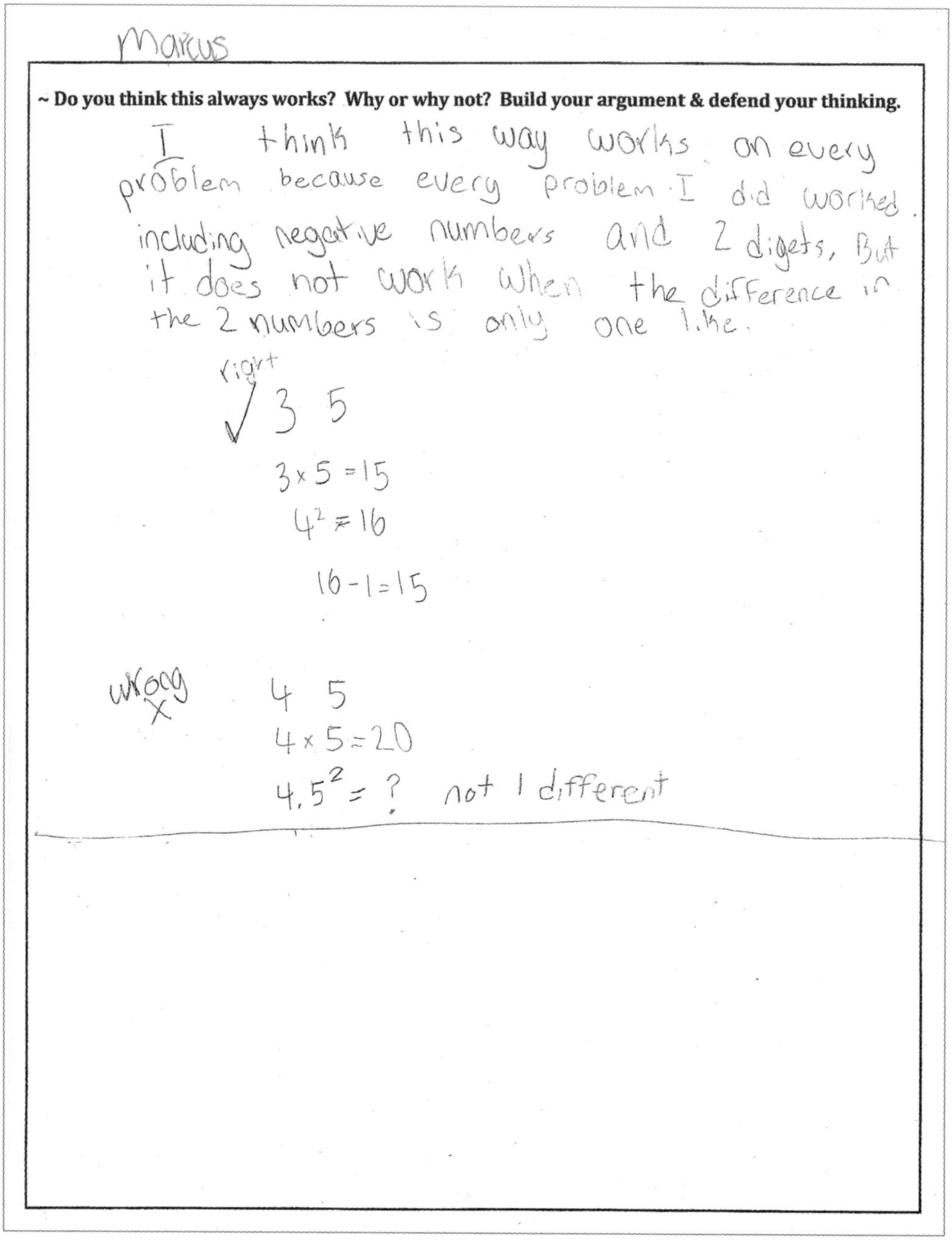

Marcus

~ **Do you think this always works? Why or why not? Build your argument & defend your thinking.**

I think this way works on every problem because every problem I did worked. including negative numbers and 2 digets, But it does not work when the difference in the 2 numbers is only one like.

right

√ 3 5

$3 \times 5 = 15$

$4^2 = 16$

$16 - 1 = 15$

wrong
X

4 5

$4 \times 5 = 20$

$4.5^2 = ?$ not 1 different

of something mathematical from this perspective. They were given a series of steps to follow and then asked to see what they could see. What I could see right away for some of my students was panic; they clearly thought that they could not even start to solve it. With a little scaffolding, however, they pushed onward and found out it was not too far beyond them. They then did well in expressing regularity in repeated reasoning once they were able to find the patterns within the work, and once they did, the door was open. I did see that what most of them observed came through their calculations and not from doing it out with tiles. I think they were fairly confident in their reasoning that the arithmetic part worked, but I don't think many of them saw it as deeply connected to the mathematics under the task of how and why a square of tiles can no longer remain a square if one tile is removed, and how this relates to the dimensions of the newly formed rectangle. This is a problem I would like to revisit.

▶ MP8 Reflection

There is no question that this MP is the one I feel least comfortable with, for a variety of reasons. First of all, it is hard even to remember the words in the title of it. Regularity in Repeated Reasoning is not something I ever remember being taught when I was an elementary, middle, or even high school student. I also don't remember learning about it in college, so I don't think I have actively put it out there in my classroom. I think that I have to break down the words more carefully for myself as well as for my students. If I don't, I'm afraid that they are just nice words without meaning.

COMMENTS ABOUT MP8 FROM OTHER CLASSROOM TEACHERS

Grade Two Teacher: Not long ago, I basically knew nothing about any of the MPs. Yes, I had heard of the Common Core, but the Mathematical Practices as part of the Common Core were not something I knew. The MPs were basically a bunch of jargon to me at first. I had no idea how they fit, nor did I want to think about how I was going to translate all of this technical math language in a way to make it accessible to my second graders. This was especially true about MP8. I understand repeated reasoning. I understand how looking for patterns is helpful. I did support this a bit more specifically in our geometry unit by discussing attributes, their similarities and differences, and how that can lead to pattern identification. I addressed it a bit in our work with computational methods. Overall, however, I do not feel as if I fully taught this practice. Next year, I hope to expand my teaching and integration of MP8.

Grade Five Teacher: Even when I am with other teachers who are working as hard as I am in trying to integrate the Mathematical Practices into the classroom, I don't know anyone who really and truly gets this MP completely yet. I think that I have to make all of the MPs, and certainly this one, into a natural language—meaning that it is used every day. I believe that this will happen if kids are involved in the roll-out process and if I have them work at creating and adjusting their meanings and understandings of the MPs as we move through the year.

COMMENTS ABOUT MP8 FROM STUDENTS

Bethuel, Kindergarten Student: This repeats all the time. When we add one more sticker for every day in school, the blank spaces in the ten frames get one less. It's a pattern!

Rudy, Grade Two Student: This MP is important because if you have a very hard problem, you can use what you know to solve the problem. It makes the hard problem easier and makes me not give up.

Cameron, Grade Three Student: This is about turning the problem into something you saw before and seeing the regular part of it. Division is repeated subtraction and times is repeated addition, and the easier ones help with the harder ones.

The only way to make sense out of change is to plunge into it, move with it, and join the dance.

—*ALAN WATTS*, THE WISDOM OF INSECURITY

So just how do you go about joining this dance of change trumpeted by the Common Core? How do you plunge in and start or continue to make sense of the Mathematical Practices for yourself? How do you move forward with what you know about the MPs and integrate that into your daily practice? How do you learn the steps of the dance and make the MPs explicit to yourself? How do you make them explicit to your students? Where do you begin?

Let's begin with reviewing some basic tenets related to the Mathematical Practices and how you can make sense of them and tap into their power. After that there are a few more specific suggestions about your next steps. Finally, there is a list of resources to help you keep on dancing!

Basic Tenets of the Common Core Mathematical Practices

The Mathematical Practices

1. are meant for all students;

2. can be taught;

3. must be taught;

4. are not discrete and often overlap with and blend into each other;

5. are not all present in every lesson;

6. take time for teachers to make sense of, to understand, and to implement;

7. develop over time in students; and

8. reside at the core of mathematical proficiency.

Here are a few thoughts about each of these tenets:

1. The Mathematical Practices are meant as a way of approaching and thinking about mathematics for every student at every grade and ability level. They are not reserved for "higher-achieving" students only, and they must be thought of as attainable ways of thinking for all of our students.

2. The MPs can be taught but only if they are made both "explicit and learnable," a phrase Deborah Ball used at the National Council of Supervisors of Mathematics Annual Meeting in 2012. I couldn't agree with this statement more! They are not necessarily instinctive and need to be overt and transparent so that students are aware of what they are and can be taught how to use them.

3. The MPs must be taught and must be taught in an integrated way. They are not to be thought of as something separate from mathematical content, but rather as a way to access mathematical content. Susan Jo Russell maintains that although we have to focus in on the MPs "with targeted, intentional, planned instruction," we need to be careful that they are not "relegated to special sessions apart from core mathematical content; they are necessarily embedded in content" (2012, 52).

4. There will be evidence of multiple MPs within every lesson. It would be hard to construct a viable argument (MP3), for example, without being precise in the use of language, mathematical symbols, diagrams, and so on (MP6). Further, it may be difficult to see a clear line between which of the Mathematical Practices are at work, because they often—and should—seep into one another.

5. I have often heard that "We do all of the Mathematical Practices in every lesson." Although more than one MP is typically present in every lesson, it is very rare that all eight MPs are at play. It is far more likely that there are one or two "focus" Mathematical Practices, ones that are more visible and are highlighted within the lesson to a greater degree.

6. Teachers and administrators need to acknowledge that full understanding of the Mathematical Practices is going to take time. The process of making sense of the MPs is a multifaceted, multidimensional one and evolves over time. With this acknowledgment comes permission to start the dance without knowing all of the steps, to try some things out, to feel the rhythm, so to speak, and to recognize that with practice, the quality of the dance improves.

7. Just as making sense of the MPs takes time for teachers, it takes time to develop in students. One of the most promising elements of the Mathematical Practices is that there are only eight of them and that they are *common* to all students from kindergarten through grade twelve. This means that when (note that I am saying *when*, not *if*) all teachers tuck the MPs into their daily practice, students will grow in their use of them as they grow from kindergartners to high school seniors. What an amazing thought!

8. This is it—this is the crux of what we are striving for in mathematics education: mathematical proficiency for all students. When students are adept and skilled in problem solving and building arguments, and identifying structure and using patterns, and all the other wonderful elements of the Mathematical Practices, they will be mathematically proficient and capable of thinking deeply and tapping into their power.

Possible Steps

1. Self-Assessment:

   - Try this activity on your own and see what you can determine about your knowledge and understanding of the Mathematical Practices. Get a piece of blank paper (8½ by 11 inches is fine). Fold the paper into fourths (fold into halves one way; keep it folded and then fold that in half the other way). Label the four boxes on the front 1–4 and the four on the back 5–8. Now name the eight MPs and write what you know about each of them.

- Look over what you have written and use the GOLD framework. See if you have identified at least one G—goal—for each MP. Check to see if you have written about what actions you might be O—observing students engage in, what words you might be L—listening for students to say, and what actions you might be D—doing to foster the growth and use of the MPs.

- Consider doing this activity with a grade-level colleague from your school, someone on your grade-level team, a teacher from a grade below and/or above yours, a teacher or teachers from another school, and so on.

2. Collaborative Study:

- Construct a partnership or team of colleagues who want to engage in further exploration of the Mathematical Practices. You may opt for working with one partner, a triad, or a larger group. Determine the type of collaboration you wish to engage in together; peer coaching and professional learning communities (PLCs) are possibilities.
  - Determine if peer coaching is the approach you want. It is one way for you to collaborate where you can work with a trusted colleague, agree to meet together on a regular basis, discuss a specific MP, observe each other with a focus on the chosen MP, give feedback, offer suggestions, and so on.
  - Consider professional learning communities. They are another and more formal way for you to collaborate with peers. With a central goal of improving student learning, PLCs are a powerful force and a perfect fit to help make sense of the Mathematical Practices.

- Limit the scope of your initial work. Do not set as a goal that you will fully make sense of, understand deeply, implement, and integrate seamlessly all eight MPs in one year. Allow yourself time to study, assimilate, and "practice" a few of the MPs at a time.

3. Administrative Support:

- Approach your building and/or district mathematics specialist, curriculum director, math coach—any and all of them if you have them within your reach. Ask to meet with them about your specific goal centered on the Mathematical Practices. Ask them to think about providing extended, targeted, and ongoing professional development on the MPs. Invite them into your classroom to model and observe.

- Speak to your building principal about your plans. Share your specific MP goals and think about rolling them into your formal professional development plan. Ask for opportunities to get into other classrooms and/or other schools with the explicit purpose of observing the MPs in practice.

RECOMMENDED ONLINE RESOURCES

This is not an exhaustive list, but it does provide a place to begin.

1. http://commoncore.americaachieves.org
   America Achieves is another site that houses videos that depict how the key shifts found in the Common Core can and do come to life in classrooms. In addition to lesson videos, you will find videos of teachers discussing their lessons as well as links to other resources.

2. http://mathpractices.edc.org
   This site is under the umbrella of the Education Development Center (EDC). The EDC has expanded its work since its inception and is considered a front-runner in the melding of research and practice in education. This particular site is focused on the connection between the MPs and the content standards and offers multiple illustrations, all of which revolve around student dialogues and allow the viewer to see the MPs as they play out in classrooms.

3. www.illustrativemathematics.org
   The mission of this collective body of committed educators is to provide and share "carefully vetted resources for teachers and teacher leaders" so that both the teaching and learning of mathematics will be improved. It is headed by Bill McCallum, one of the lead writers of the CCSS for Mathematics. The resources within this site are vast, so take some time to peruse. Although work is still continuing on the illustrations of the MPs as well as on the commentary and elaborations by grade band, the site is a powerhouse of information.

4. www.corestandards.org/resources
   This site is from the Common Core State Standards Initiative. It provides a history of the development of the CCSS, as well as an overview, the specific standards, frequently asked questions and their answers, and many other important resources.

5. www.insidemathematics.org
   Inside Mathematics is a resource open to educators worldwide to help them in their quest to provide the best mathematics instruction possible. Within this resource, there are video examples of the Mathematical Practices excerpted from a range of grade levels.

6. www.teachingchannel.org/videos/
   The Teaching Channel is all about "great teaching" and "inspiring classrooms." It offers a collection of videos that showcase successful teaching practices across America and across various content areas. You won't be sorry if you check out the videos housed here.

FINAL WORDS

Now it is up to you to join the dance. There is no doubt that change is messy and presents challenges. There is no doubt that making sense of the Common Core Mathematical Practices will take time and effort. There is also no doubt, however, that what lies ahead for our students is a world that will require them to be the kinds of thinkers who use the types of thinking encapsulated in the Mathematical Practices. Having a good memory and being able to recall information will not be quite as valuable. What will be needed are people who, according to David Brooks in a 2014 *New York Times* op-ed column, "possess a voracious explanatory drive, an almost obsessive need to follow their curiosity," so that they engage in "extended bouts of concentration, diving into and trying to make sense of [these] bottomless information oceans" (Brooks 2014). Although the Mathematical Practices do not promote obsessive behavior, they most certainly do promote the development and use of higher-order levels of thinking. They are packed with the power that our students will need to face the future and meet the challenges ahead of them.

REFERENCES

Anderson, Lorin W., David R. Krathwohl, Peter W. Airasian, Kathleen A. Cruikshank, Richard E. Mayer, Paul R. Pintrich, James Raths, and Merlin C. Wittrock. 2001. *A Taxonomy for Learning, Teaching, and Assessing: A Revision of Bloom's Taxonomy of Educational Objectives*. New York: Pearson, Allyn & Bacon.

Barlow, Angela T., and Michael R. McCrory. 2011. "3 Strategies for Promoting Math Disagreements." *Teaching Children Mathematics* 17 (9): 530–539.

Ball, Deborah Loewenberg. 2012. "Practicing the Common Core: What Is the Work of Teaching?" Paper presented at the annual meeting of the National Council of Supervisors of Mathematics, Philadelphia, April.

Bloom, Benjamin S. 1956. *Taxonomy of Educational Objectives, Handbook 1: The Cognitive Domain*. New York: David McKay.

Bond, Rebecca. 2004. *This Place in the Snow*. New York: Dutton Children's Books.

Brooks, David. 2014. "Op-ed." *New York Times*, February 2.

Carpenter, Thomas P., and Linda Levi. 1999. "Developing Conceptions of Algebraic Reasoning in the Primary Grades." Paper presented at the annual meeting of the American Educational Research Association, Montreal, April.

Carpenter, Thomas P., Linda Levi, Megan Loef Franke, and Julie Koehler Zeringue. 2005. "Algebra in Elementary School: Developing Relational Thinking." *ZDM: The International Journal on Mathematics Education* 7 (3): 231–317.

Chapin, Suzanne H., Catherine O'Connor, and Nancy Canavan Anderson. 2009. *Classroom Discussions: Using Math Talk to Help Students Learn*. Sausalito, CA: Math Solutions.

Dacey, Linda, Jane Bamford Lynch, and Rebeka Eston Salemi. 2013. *How to Differentiate Your Math Instruction: Lessons, Ideas, and Videos with Common Core Support*. Sausalito, CA: Math Solutions.

Duncker, Karl. 1945. "On Problem Solving." *Psychological Monographs* 58 (5): i–113.

Fennell, Francis, and Theodore E. Landis. 1994. "Number and Operation Sense." In *Windows of Opportunity: Mathematics for Students with Special Needs*, ed. C. A. Thornton and N. S. Bley. Reston, VA: National Council of Teachers of Mathematics.

Greenes, Carole E., Carol R. Findell, M. Katherine Gavin, and Linda Jensen Sheffield. 2000. *Awesome Math Problems for Creative Thinking.* Chicago: Creative.

Hoogeboom, Shirley, and Judy Goodnow. 2004. *Problem Solver II.* Chicago:

Wright Group McGraw-Hill.

Illustrative Mathematics. 2014. *Standards for Mathematical Practice: Commentary and Elaborations for K–5.* Tucson, Arizona. http://commoncoretools.me/wp-content/uploads/2014/02/Elaborations.pdf.

Kanold, Timothy D., ed. 2012. *Common Core Mathematics in a PLC at Work, Grades* K–2. Bloomington, IL: Solution Tree Press.

Kazemi, Elham, and Allison Hintz. 2014. *Intentional Talk: How to Structure and Lead Productive Mathematical Discussions.* Portland, ME: Stenhouse.

Lannin, John K. 2005. "Generalization and Justification: The Challenge of Introducing Algebraic Reasoning through Pattern Activities." *Mathematical Thinking and Learning* 7 (3): 231–317.

Lent, ReLeah Cossett. 2012. *Overcoming Textbook Fatigue: 21st Century Tools to Revitalize Teaching and Learning.* Alexandria, VA: Association for Supervision and Curriculum Development.

McGarvey, Lynn M. 2013. "Is It a Pattern?" *Teaching Children Mathematics* 19 (9): 564.

Meehan, Robert John. 2010. *The Teacher's Journey: The Road Less Traveled.* Mustang, OK: Tate.

Moynihan, Christine. 2013. "Leadership Tips." *NCSM Newsletter* 44 (1): 20–21.

National Council of Teachers of Mathematics. 2000. *Principles and Standards for School Mathematics.* Reston, VA: National Council of Teachers of Mathematics.

———. 2014. *Principles to Actions: Ensuring Mathematical Success for All.* Reston, VA: National Council of Teachers of Mathematics.

National Governors Association Center for Best Practices, Council of Chief State School Officers. 2010. *Common Core State Standards Mathematics.* Washington, DC: National Governors Association Center for Best Practices, Council of Chief State School Officers.

Polya, George. 1945. *How to Solve It.* Princeton, NJ: Princeton University Press.

Ritchie, Anne Thackeray. 1885. *Mrs. Dymond.* Cambridge, MA: Harvard University.

Rollins, Suzy Pepper. 2014. *Learning in the Fast Lane: 8 Ways to Put All Students on the Road to Academic Success.* Alexandria, VA: Association for Supervision and Curriculum Development.

Rusczyk, Richard. 2012. Founder of Art of Problem Solving. http://www.artofproblemsolving.com/Wiki/index.php?title=Problem_solving&direction=next&oldid=47735.

Russell, Susan Jo. 2000. "Principles and Standards: Developing Computational Fluency with Whole Numbers." *Teaching Children Mathematics* 7 (3): 154–158.

———. 2012. "CCSSM: Keeping Teaching and Learning Strong." *Teaching Children Mathematics* 19 (1): 50–56.

Schoenfeld, Alan H. 1994. *Mathematical Thinking and Problem Solving*. Hillsdale, NJ: Lawrence Erlbaum.

Seeley, Cathy L. 2014. *Smarter Than We Think: More Messages About Math, Teaching, and Learning in the 21st Century*. Sausalito, CA: Math Solutions.

Seuss, Dr. 1940. *Horton Hatches the Egg*. New York: Random House.

Sousa, David A. 2008. *How the Brain Learns Mathematics*: Thousand Oaks, CA: Corwin Press.

Tapper, John. 2012. *Solving for Why: Understanding, Assessing, and Teaching Students Who Struggle with Math*. Sausalito, CA: Math Solutions.

Varlas, Laura. 2012. "Academic Vocabulary Builds Student Achievement." *ASCD Education Update* 54 (11): 1–5.

Wagner, Tony. 2008. *The Global Achievement Gap: Why Even Our Best Schools Don't Teach the New Survival Skills Our Children Need—and What We Can Do About It*. New York: Basic Books.

Watts, Alan. 2011. *The Wisdom of Insecurity: A Message for an Age of Anxiety.* 2nd ed. New York: Vintage Books.

Wedekind, Kassia Omohundro. 2011. *Math Exchanges: Guiding Young Mathematicians in Small-Group Meetings*. Portland, ME: Stenhouse.

INDEX

Page numbers followed by an *f* indicate figures.

A

abstract reasoning. *See also* MP2: Reason Abstractly and Quantitatively; reasoning
  classroom lesson, 31–38, 33*f*, 35*f*, 36*f*, 48–55, 51*f*, 52*f*, 53*f*
  mathematical modeling, 57
  overview, 23, 26
administrative support, 151
Anderson, Lorin, 2
arguments. See also MP3: Construct Viable Arguments and Critique the Reasoning of Others
  classroom lesson, 48–55, 51*f*, 52*f*, 53*f*
  mathematical tools and, 62
  overview, 41
Awesome Math Problems for Creative Thinking, 48

B

background knowledge, 115–117, 116*f*
Ball, Deborah, 148
Barlow, Angela, 62
base ten, 64–74, 67*f*, 68*f*, 69*f*, 70*f*, 71*f*
Bloom, Benjamin, 2

Bond, Rebecca, 84
Brooks, David, 153

C

calculations
  MP6: Attend to Precision, 100–102, 101*f*
  repetitions in, 128–130, 129*f*
Carpenter, Thomas, 130
change, process of, 2, 147–151
collaborative study of the Mathematical Practices, 150
Common Core State Standards (CCSS)
  in general, 1. *See also* Mathematical Practices (MPs)
communication. *See also* MP3: Construct Viable Arguments and Critique the Reasoning of Others; MP6: Attend to Precision
  mathematically specific language, 96–98, 97*f*, 109
  overview, 41, 95–96
  symbols and labels and, 98–100, 99*f*
complex problems, 60, 62
computational fluency
  MP6: Attend to Precision, 100–102, 101*f*
  repetitions in, 128–130, 129*f*
connections, 80–82, 81*f*
contextualization, 28–30, 29*f*